Scripture, Ethics, and the
Possibility of Same-Sex Relationships

Scripture, Ethics, and the Possibility of Same-Sex Relationships

Karen R. Keen

WM. B. EERDMANS PUBLISHING COMPANY
GRAND RAPIDS, MICHIGAN

Wm. B. Eerdmans Publishing Co.
4035 Park East Court SE, Grand Rapids, Michigan 49546
www.eerdmans.com

27 26 25 24 23   11 12 13 14

ISBN 978-0-8028-7654-6

Library of Congress Cataloging-in-Publication Data

Names: Keen, Karen R., 1973- author.
Title: Scripture, ethics, and the possibility of same-sex relationships /
    Karen R. Keen.
Description: Grand Rapids : Eerdmans Publishing Co., 2018. |
    Includes bibliographical references.
Identifiers: LCCN 2018022305 | ISBN 9780802876546 (pbk. : alk. paper)
Subjects: LCSH: Homosexuality—Religious aspects—Christianity.
Classification: LCC BR115.H6 K44 2018 | DDC 261.8/35766—dc23
LC record available at https://lccn.loc.gov/2018022305

In memory of
Ryan Robertson
(1989–2009)

And to his loving parents,
Rob and Linda

"Just because he breathes"
justbecausehebreathes.com

Contents

Preface   ix

1. The Church's Response to the Gay and
   Lesbian Community: A Brief History   1

2. Same-Sex Relations in Ancient
   Jewish and Christian Thought   16

3. Key Arguments in Today's Debate
   on Same-Sex Relationships   25

4. Fifty Shekels for Rape? Making Sense
   of Old Testament Laws   43

5. What Is Ethical? Interpreting the Bible like Jesus   54

6. The Question of Celibacy for
   Gay and Lesbian People   68

7. Is It Adam's Fault? Why the Origin
   of Same-Sex Attraction Matters   83

8. Imagining a New Response to the
   Gay and Lesbian Community   101

CONTENTS

Notes	115
Acknowledgments	140
Subject-Name Index	142
Scripture Index	146

Preface

Over the Christmas holiday last year, my sister and I were driving to an antique shop with teenage nieces in the back seat when she turned to me and asked, "Did you know Christian writer Jen Hatmaker supports gay marriage now? I don't understand her theology. Can you explain it?" I was grateful for her question and desire to learn more about a challenging topic. The evangelical world is facing increasing tension as leaders like Hatmaker express affirmation of same-sex relationships. Last year, the internet exploded over influential pastor Eugene Peterson's statement that he would officiate a gay marriage. The author of *The Message* Bible translation quickly recanted in the face of negative publicity. So, what is causing some Christians to switch sides in the debate? I wrote this book for those like my sister who want to better understand the answer to that question.

I also wrote this book for those who find themselves in my shoes. These pages reflect years of prayer and study as I have sought personal direction. That search started in my late teens when I consciously admitted to myself that I am gay. For a girl who was raised a conservative Baptist from the cradle, that was a terrifying realization. How was it even possible? I had always been taught that gay and lesbian people are unbelievers outside the church. I was a devout Christian who dreamed of being a missionary like my hero, Amy Carmichael.

That experience awakened me to the reality that not everything is as simple as what I learned in Sunday school. My presuppositions about God were shaken. For several years, I was racked with grief and confusion. But eventually I reached a place of spiritual peace. I resigned myself to a celibate life and focused on serving in ministry. I went to seminary and on to postgraduate work in biblical studies. Then something happened. The more I dug deep into the Bible, the more I felt a gnawing sense that my previous conclusions were incomplete. New questions arose that I had not considered before.

As I continued to pray and study, I increasingly came to the views that I present in this book.* I found that Scripture offers a life-giving vision I had not seen before. The conclusions I draw do not come out of attempts to rationalize my own desire for a same-sex relationship. As I write this preface, I have been living celibate for sixteen years. Indeed, there is no woman in sight. I don't know what the future holds for me relationally, but I walk into it with open palms.

In the following pages, I take you on the journey I have traveled in the search for truth. In Chapter 1, I show you the history of the church's response to the gay and lesbian community. Our theological views are affected not only by what we read in the Bible but also by the interactions we have with people. In the past, many Christians believed false stereotypes that badly mischaracterized gay people. These ghost stories are finally being put to rest as more gay and lesbian people find the courage to share their lives with Christian friends and family. As our knowledge of human sexuality and sexual orientation increases, I suspect we will continue to grow in our pastoral responses.

In Chapter 2, I take you back in time to the land of Israel. What did the biblical authors believe about same-sex relationships and why? To understand what the Bible says, we will explore the inspired authors' intended meaning. From there, in Chapter 3, I present the most compelling arguments in the debate from both the traditionalist and the progressive points of view.

In Chapter 4, I shift gears from clarifying the foundational issues presented in the first three chapters to laying out my own arguments. This chapter addresses common confusion when it comes to interpreting the Bible. Specifically, how do we make sense of Old Testament laws, and when do we apply them to our own lives? Is the Levitical law against male-male sexual intercourse still binding?

Chapters 5 and 6 are where the rubber meets the road. In Chapter 5, I discuss the question of how we determine God's will from the Bible. In what ways does the Bible inform our ethical practice? To explore this, I turn to the biblical authors themselves to see how they interpret scriptural texts for ethics. In Chapter 6, I invite you to consider the implications of mandatory lifelong celibacy for gay and lesbian people. Is lifelong celibacy possible for everyone who attempts it?

In Chapter 7 I consider the effects of the fall in light of scientific evidence. Is same-sex attraction a symptom of evil desire, a medical condition, or simply representative of human variation in sexual development? Finally, in Chapter 8, I discuss suggestions for moving forward. How might the church reimagine its response to the gay and lesbian community?

My hope is that these chapters will be life-giving. I want to take the conversation beyond its current stalemate to help Christians contemplate new ways of thinking about this controversial topic. I also desire to equip pastors, counselors, and other church leaders who are looking for biblically sound guidance on same-sex relationships. Last but not least, I hope this book will encourage the hearts of gay and lesbian people who often feel painfully torn between faith and sexuality.

KAREN R. KEEN, ThM
Durham, North Carolina
August 2017

1

The Church's Response to the Gay and Lesbian Community: A Brief History

When it comes to same-sex relationships, there's one thing we cannot forget: *people.* The conversation is about more than doctrinal debates and biblical interpretation. It encompasses the church's response to gay and lesbian people as holistic individuals with hearts and minds and dreams.[1] This requires challenging false caricatures. How does the church understand and perceive gay people? What kinds of stories does the church tell about those who experience same-sex attraction? Perceptions about why people have such attractions or their motives for being in same-sex relationships significantly affect the treatment of gay and lesbian people. So, before jumping into the biblical debate, let's look at the church's response, especially within our own context in the last fifty years. The body of Christ can better see the way forward when it examines its own attitudes and actions within historical trends.

Until the twentieth century, the church primarily viewed those with same-sex attraction as spiritually corrupt.[2] Fourth-century theologian John Chrysostom provides a common perspective: "No one can say that it was by being prevented from legitimate intercourse that they came to this pass or that it was from having no means to fulfill their desire that they were driven to this monstrous insanity."[3] Chrysostom assumed that people engaging in same-sex relations also experienced heterosexual desire and thus could take advantage of heterosexual marriage for sexual release. He considered the cause of same-sex attraction to be "excess that cannot contain itself." Pointing to terminology in Romans 1, he argued that those who have same-sex relations are motivated not by love but by uncontrolled lust.[4]

Chrysostom's assumption of spiritual depravity is also evident in the writings of Reformer Martin Luther. He believed same-sex attraction resulted from a person turning away from God, allowing the devil to exert pressure that "extinguishes the fire of natural desire and stirs up another, which is contrary to nature."[5] The seventeenth-century minister and Bible commentator Matthew Henry said same-sex relations are "not to be mentioned without horror."[6] He believed God gave people over to "vile affections" as punishment for idolatry. He also commented with apparent approval that these individuals were being sentenced to death by his own government.

The perception of spiritual depravity persisted despite scientific hypotheses—dating to antiquity—that offered explanations for people's same-sex desire.[7] Some early Christian theologians likely rejected these hypotheses outright. First-century Jewish philosopher Philo dismissed Plato's account of innate etiology, arguing that the idea should be treated with "supreme contempt" by "disciples of Moses" who "love the truth."[8] Church fathers who knew of scientific hypotheses, as Clement of Alexandria did, continued to emphasize spiritual depravity regardless.[9] Clement believed the condition could be cured by Christ's exhortations.[10] Notably, ancient medical theories often characterized same-sex desire in negative terms of excess, disease, and mental illness.[11] Thus, rather than challenging the notion of spiritual depravity, medical diagnoses dovetailed with perceptions of a wayward personality.[12]

The trend of treating same-sex attraction as a spiritual or medical disorder continued into the nineteenth and twentieth centuries.[13] Just as ancient scholars diagnosed and categorized people, so also scientists in the modern era offered explanations of mental illness and disease. However, an important shift began to occur in the early to mid-1900s. New research on the human body offered alternative explanations to mental illness. Neuroendocrinologist Eugen Steinach (1861–1944) hypothesized that a person is gay because of the impact of sex hormones on the central nervous system.[14] Similarly, psychological studies began to show that gay people are not mentally ill by virtue of being gay.[15] This seems to have had an impact on at least some Christians who realized same-sex attraction cannot be simplistically characterized as moral corruption or even something that can be cured.

One such thinker was C. S. Lewis. In a 1953 letter to a friend, he suggested gay people have a lifelong condition and declined to offer spiritual explanations for causation. He still believed same-sex attraction was a kind of disability, but rather than a cure, he suggested gay people could find redemptive purpose in their lot: "Our speculations on the cause of the abnormality are not what matters and we must be content with ignorance. The disciples were not told why (in terms of efficient cause) the man was born blind (Jn. IX 1–3): only the final cause, that the works of God should be made manifest in him. This suggests that in homosexuality, as in every other tribulation, those works can be made manifest: i.e. that every disability conceals a vocation, if only we can find it."[16]

Lewis was before his time, and it would be many years before the church at large caught up with him. But others were also rethinking the issue. Notably, gay and lesbian people themselves began challenging both ancient and modern theories of disorder, testifying that their lives did not match prevailing negative assumptions. This shift accelerated during the countercultural movements of the 1960s. Tired of constant police raids on gay establishments, the famous 1969 Stonewall rioters launched a visible fight for dignity and fair treatment. Shortly thereafter, in 1972, the United Church of Christ began ordaining gay and lesbian pastors, the first mainline denomination to do so.[17]

Five Stages in the Conservative Church's Response
to Gay and Lesbian People

While some progressive Christians began affirming gay and lesbian people in the twentieth century, much of the church remained conservative on the matter. In the rest of this chapter I will unpack historical trends from the 1960s to the present. The conservative church's response can be summarized in five stages. These stages represent a chronological trajectory, but all can be found simultaneously across various churches today.

1. "Gay people should stay in the closet."

Prior to the 1960s, few gay or lesbian people were willing to risk telling anyone about their sexual orientation. James White and Jeffrey Niell write approvingly of this closet: "In the past homosexuals were ashamed to 'go public.' Historically, theologians were not required to address this topic as it was commonly understood to be a violation of God's law."[18] Many churchgoers have found public discussion and theological inquiry of sexuality threatening and uncomfortable, preferring that gay people live in secrecy.

2. "Gay people are perverts and criminals."

After the Stonewall riots in 1969, the church could no longer ignore the reality of gay and lesbian people. However, aside from rare exceptions like the United Church of Christ, most Christians viewed sexual minorities as godless and rebellious individuals who willfully engaged in perverted and criminal behavior. Few conservatives could conceive of gay people as potential Christians deeply devoted to their faith. Many writers portrayed sexual minorities as pedophiles, addicts, mentally disturbed people, promiscuous deviants, or even Nazis. Gay people were to be feared as dangerous.

Alan Sears and Craig Osten described orgies that made it unsafe "to go to the forest, where just thirty years ago, families and civic groups were able to innocently enjoy its natural beauty."[19] They warned their readers not to humanize gay people as "just like my fishing buddy." Similarly, Michael Pakaluk justified job discrimination by painting sexual minorities as deficient in character, lacking "the virtue of self-control" and "insight into some basic human goods."[20] The most notorious portrait has been promoted by speaker and writer Scott Lively, who associates gay people with serial killers and Nazis.[21]

Demeaning characterizations have also come from "friendly" sources. Dr. Joseph Nicolosi, a Catholic psychologist who claimed to provide compassionate therapy, compared gay people to Scar in *The Lion King*, "the brooding, resentful brother of the King [who] lives his life on the margins of society and is full of envy and anger."[22] Nicolosi writes, "Scar ruptures the link between the generations by killing the Lion King and aligning himself with a scavenger pack of hyenas. Thus, Scar turns the ordered lion kingdom into chaos and ruin. Before all this occurs, however, we hear a brief, light-hearted exchange between the young male cub, Simba, and his uncle Scar. Laughingly, Simba says, 'Uncle Scar, you're weird.' Meaningfully, Scar replies, 'You have no idea.'"[23]

Not surprisingly, such an understanding has fostered treating gay and lesbian people as criminals. Pakaluk writes, "Anti-sodomy laws have a valuable function. . . . They constitute a kind of link with the past, a link to society as it was before the sexual revolution, when our insight into matters sexual was clearer."[24] Notably, imprisonment of gay people was legal in the United States as recently as 2003.[25]

3. "Gay people are hapless victims who need healing."

While the criminal/pervert caricature endured into the early 2000s, a new paradigm simultaneously developed in the 1990s: the gay person as a broken struggler in need of compassion. This change in perception was the result of the ex-gay movement's impact on the conservative church. The movement began in the 1970s but was largely ignored until the 1990s.[26] Its existence was possible because, after Stonewall, gay people experienced increasing freedom to speak openly about their lives. Previously, people stayed silent out of fear of persecution. But now Christians distressed by their own sexuality were risking self-disclosure to seek help.

In 1973 the father of the ex-gay movement, Frank Worthen, started a ministry near San Francisco called Love in Action. Worthen had lived as a gay man for twenty-five years before having a spiritual experience that led him to renounce same-sex relationships and marry a woman. He founded his ministry to help others who wanted to live congruently with their traditionalist interpretation of the Bible. In 1975 he discovered other fledgling ex-gay ministries, including one called EXIT (Ex-Gay Intervention Team) that operated out of Melodyland Christian Center, founded by two gay men in their twenties, Michael Bussee and Jim Kasper.

Worthen collaborated with EXIT to host the first ex-gay conference, which was attended by sixty-five people (sixty men and five women).[27] This conference birthed Exodus International, an information and referral organization that eventually grew to more than two hundred member ministries worldwide. (Exodus thrived until its closure in 2013, when then president Alan Chambers shocked conservatives and progressives alike by admitting that the majority of ex-gays had not experienced change in their sexual orientation despite the efforts of Exodus.)

Members of Exodus International believed that it was possible to change one's sexual orientation by submitting to Christ and addressing childhood wounds. Books like *You Don't Have to Be*

Gay and *Coming Out of Homosexuality: New Freedom for Men and Women* offered hope of heterosexuality. In *You Don't Have to Be Gay*, Jeff Konrad writes, "Despite what we hear from the media and the world at large, your homosexual orientation can be changed. . . . You will discover that a man of any age really doesn't have to be gay if he doesn't want to be."[28] Konrad and other ex-gays drew heavily on Dr. Elizabeth Moberly's theories of gender identity confusion and rupture in parent-child relationships. The approach encouraged gay men to embrace their masculinity and lesbians to accept their femininity. In doing so, a man could feel like "one of the guys" and a woman like "one of the ladies," thereby preventing the eroticization of the same sex as "other."

In 1992 Benjamin Kaufman, MD, Charles Socarides, MD, and Dr. Joseph Nicolosi founded the National Association for Research and Therapy of Homosexuality (NARTH), which advanced and expanded on Moberly's theories. NARTH labeled its approach "reparative therapy." This method aimed to correct a person's attempts to self-repair gender inferiority and childhood trauma via homosexual relationships. In a well-known refrain advising parents on preventing homosexuality, Nicolosi said, "We advise fathers, 'If you don't hug your sons, some other man will.'" Nicolosi has given various success rates for reparative therapy, including approximately 30 percent. However, NARTH has been hampered by its lack of peer-reviewed research to back its claims.

Surprisingly, the early ex-gay movement had little support from churches, even with its adherence to a traditional sexual ethic. The stigma around homosexuality was so pronounced that conservative churches didn't want anything to do with gay people—even those who wanted help becoming heterosexual. Worthen recalls, "Initially, all our opposition came from the Christian community, rather than the gay community. . . . It will take the church about one hundred years to really understand what we're doing."[29]

However, the ex-gay movement gained traction in 1998 when Focus on the Family joined hands with ex-gay leaders to create the

Love Won Out conference, a platform that paradoxically preached compassion for gay people while promoting strategies to fight gay rights. Focus was one of the first major Christian organizations to collaborate with ex-gay ministries, lending credibility to the movement. Exodus benefited from the alliance, but it came with a price. The Religious Right wanted to use ex-gay testimonies to fight political battles. Gay rights hinged on the assertion that sexual orientation is immutable and akin to race and gender. Thus, the ex-gay movement, which had focused primarily on pastoral care, now became politicized.

Religious Right organizations recruited ex-gays to testify in Washington, D.C., to counter gay-rights efforts. Full-page ads were placed in prominent newspapers across the country proclaiming that change is possible. The psychological theory that same-sex attraction is environmentally caused, and therefore treatable, was no longer championed merely to provide compassionate help, but also to shape legislation. Any research which suggested that change is not possible was (and still is) refuted by the Religious Right. To concede that sexual orientation may be immutable for some people is to lose the political battle.

Despite the political entanglements, the collaboration with Focus on the Family created a larger platform for ex-gays. For the first time, many churchgoers heard stories of devout Christians who experienced same-sex attraction yet desired to follow a traditional sexual ethic. Conservatives had no patience for the gay activist or gay-affirming Christian, but they could relate to the theological convictions of ex-gays. As a result, ex-gays were able to challenge the stereotype that being gay was only a rebellious behavioral choice. Ex-gays persuasively testified that they had never chosen their same-sex attraction. In response, churches became more supportive of efforts to heal or cure gay and lesbian people rather than criminalize them.

4. *"Gay people are admirable saints called to a celibate life."*

The 2000s brought another significant shift in the conservative church's response to gay and lesbian people: the awareness that sexual orientation change is unlikely for many. Like previous shifts, this was brought about by the stories of gay people, namely, young Christians whose testimonies differed from those of classic ex-gays. Ex-gay testimonies frequently cited a history of dysfunctional behavior, including promiscuity and drug abuse. Thus, reports of change in sexual orientation were enmeshed with experiences of healing from destructive habits or wounds of childhood sexual abuse. This phenomenon is captured well in the film *Save Me*.[30] In contrast, a new generation of gay Christians had benefited from societal openness and so were able to talk about and process their feelings at a younger age, prior to even having sexual relationships. These young Christians often reported growing up in loving homes and had no history of destructive behavior. They remained devoted to God and committed to chastity. The celibate gay Christian movement rejected the ex-gay movement. It challenged the notion that same-sex attractions are always caused by environmental factors and that a person's sexual orientation can change.[31]

The ex-gay movement itself eventually began to grapple with the lack of change in sexual orientation. It took a generation for the results to come in. The movement had been founded on optimism. Surely, a loving, powerful God would readily heal sinful desires and transform the life of any gay person who wanted it. Wasn't this the promise of the gospel? Significantly, the ex-gay movement was influenced by charismatic theology. The co-founders of Exodus were involved in charismatic churches when they started the organization, and other pillars of the ex-gay movement, such as Andy Comiskey, were also significantly influenced by the charismatic tradition. This theology tends to emphasize the importance of one's faith to achieve healing. If you believe God can heal you, it will happen. No one has been more long-suffering and optimistic than ex-gays who earnestly waited decades for the expected change in orientation.

But, moving into the 2010s, certain prominent leaders began to admit to themselves and others that sexual orientation change seemed to occur for only a very small percentage of people. Two of the highest-profile ex-gays who have recanted include John Paulk and John Smid. Paulk and his wife, Anne, were featured on the cover of *Newsweek* (in 1998), wrote books, and worked for Focus on the Family. However, after twenty years of marriage, they divorced in 2013. Anne remains committed to ex-gay philosophy, while John is now in a relationship with a man. Likewise, John Smid, longtime director of Love in Action (having taken over for Frank Worthen), divorced his wife in 2011 and married a man in 2014. Smid tells his story in the book *Ex'd Out: How I Fired the Shame Committee*.

The ex-gay movement was also shaken by the about-face of Exodus president Alan Chambers, which led to the organization's demise in 2013, after forty years of ministry. Chambers had come on board in 2001 and was instrumental in pulling Exodus further into Religious Right politics. However, in 2012 he declared, "The majority of people that I have met, and I would say the majority meaning 99.9% of them, have not experienced a change in their orientation or have gotten to a place where they could say that they could never be tempted or are not tempted in some way or experience some level of same-sex attraction."[32] Chambers now affirms gay marriage but remains happily married to his wife.[33] Randy Thomas, who worked alongside Chambers at Exodus for eleven years, also changed his views and is in a relationship with a man.

Awareness that sexual orientation doesn't change for the majority of gay people has led many conservative leaders to shift the focus from healing to celibacy.[34] Of course, the Catholic Church has always supported this approach, given its historically positive posture toward vowed celibacy for the priesthood. But Protestants have long championed marriage as the sign of healthy sexuality. Nevertheless, more and more evangelicals now affirm lifelong celibacy as the answer for Christians with same-sex attraction. Celibate gay Christians who lend their voices to this movement include Wesley Hill, Ron Belgau, and Eve Tushnet.[35] The group also includes gay members married to people of the opposite sex who are straight (mixed-orientation marriages), such as writers Melinda Selmys and Nathan Collins. This movement has made notable contributions to theologies of friendship and community.[36]

As traditionalists have listened to celibate gay Christians, empathy has increased. Many church leaders acknowledge the heartache that comes with unmarried life and advocate the church's role in providing supportive community. At the same time, the question of whether lifelong celibacy is possible for everyone hasn't received much attention. Instead, celibate gay Christians are held up as admirable examples of how to live a self-sacrificial life.

5. *"Gay people are _____."*

Currently, the conservative church finds itself with a palette of options. For years the ex-gay movement provided the predominant response to homosexuality. But the rise of the celibate gay movement and the demise of Exodus International disrupted this uniformity, and four key groups have emerged from this splinter:

- *Celibate gay Christians* tend to be young, ecumenical, and highly educated (albeit still predominantly white and male, as with the ex-gay movement). They are more apt to support innate explanations for causation rather than explanations pointing to social environment. Change in sexual orientation is generally not pursued (since it is believed to be hardwired). However, members are open to mixed-orientation marriages. The group emphasizes strong friendships and community. The master's- and doctoral-level training of its leaders has led to significant theological contributions on the subject. Their writings appear on the website *Spiritual Friendship* (spiritual friendship.org) And several of them have written notable books, which include Wesley Hill's *Spiritual Friendship: Finding Love in the Church as a Celibate Gay Christian* and Eve Tushnet's *Gay and Catholic: Accepting My Sexuality, Finding Community, Living My Faith.*[37]

- *Ex-gays* still have an active presence. Even though the movement died with the closing of Exodus International, two small groups developed that have kept this approach on the table. Restored Hope Network (RHN) represents the more conservative and reactionary of the two. It formed in 2012 as a break-away group from Exodus International after Chambers's views began to shift. Early on, the leadership required member ministries to sign a document stating singular loyalty. (Involvement with any other ex-gay group was prohibited.) RHN retains affinity with Religious Right politics. Anne Paulk, a prominent figure in the ex-gay movement, was elected the first president. The second group, Hope for Wholeness (HFW), resembles the ex-gay movement prior to its politicization and better represents what Exodus International was like before the late 1990s. Originally an Exodus affiliate ministry, HFW, under the guidance of president McKrae Game, created its own network in response to Chambers's new direction. Both organizations emphasize the signature traits of ex-gay philosophy: social environmental causation and healing of same-sex attraction.

- *Gospel Coalition same-sex-attracted evangelicals* are difficult to define with one term or phrase. Representatives of this group include Rosaria Butterfield, Sam Allberry, and Christopher Yuan. While not a product of the Gospel Coalition, they all have a close relationship with that organization, as well as with Southern Baptists like Russell Moore. What distinguishes them from ex-gays is their rejection of reparative therapy. While they consider change in sexual orientation possible through the sanctification process, they do not believe

change occurs for everyone. Thus, they are more likely to esteem lifelong celibacy. (Both Allberry and Yuan are single and
acknowledge continued same-sex attraction.) However, they
are distinct from celibate gay Christians in their rejection of the
term "gay" for self-reference, preferring "same-sex attracted."
They view gay identity as a social construct. They also tend to
argue for a spiritual etiology of same-sex attraction (the fall)
over biological or environmental causation.

- *Gay-affirming evangelicals* believe that same-sex partnerships
can be blessed by God. Prominent leaders in this group include
Justin Lee and Matthew Vines. Lee started the Gay Christian
Network in 2001, but evangelical support for same-sex relationships has only recently picked up steam. In 2017, the organization changed leadership and now goes by the name Q
Christian Fellowship. Over the years GCN/QCF has become
increasingly ecumenical, creating space for Progressive Christian theology alongside its original evangelical emphasis.[38] In
2013 Vines founded the Reformation Project, "a Bible-based,
Christian grassroots organization" that advocates LGBTQ
inclusion in the church. Both Lee and Vines have published
popular-level books: *Torn: Rescuing the Gospel from the Gays-
vs.-Christians Debate* (Lee, 2012) and *God and the Gay Christian* (Vines, 2014).

Gay-affirming evangelicals have gained traction through
the support of biblical scholars who are providing new arguments rooted in traditionally accepted hermeneutics. These
scholars include James Brownson (*Bible, Gender, Sexuality: Reframing the Church's Debate on Same-Sex Relationships*, 2013)
and Robert Song (*Covenant and Calling: Towards a Theology
of Same-Sex Relationships*, 2014). Significantly, the evangelical
publisher Zondervan recently printed a "two views" book on
homosexuality, acknowledging that the debate on same-sex
relationships is now an in-house evangelical argument (*Two
Views on Homosexuality, the Bible, and the Church*, 2016).

Summing It Up

Before engaging the biblical debate on same-sex relationships, the first step is to remember that the conversation affects the lives of real people. Understanding how the church has perceived and responded to gay and lesbian people provides crucial context for the broader discussion. Throughout much of history, the church has understood same-sex attraction and relationships as signs of spiritual depravity and disease. The twentieth century brought challenges to this perspective, including new research indicating that same-sex attraction is not the result of mental illness. Similarly, gay and lesbian people increasingly testified that their lives did not match these negative assumptions.

The civil rights movements of the 1960s opened doors not only for the broader gay community but also for Christians who wanted to find healing from their same-sex attraction. This led to the rise of the ex-gay movement, which influenced the conservative church's response to gay and lesbian people. Ex-gay Christians contributed a humanizing effect, raising awareness that a person's attraction to the same sex is not a matter of choice, a rebellion against God, or an indication of depravity of character.

Over time, ex-gay Christians themselves began to realize that sexual orientation is not as changeable as was once believed. As a result, numbers are now growing among celibate gay Christians as well as gay-affirming evangelicals. Adherence to ex-gay perspectives or Gospel Coalition positions will probably continue but is less likely to dominate the conversation in coming years. If historical trends continue, whatever paradigm shifts occur in the future will likely flow from gay and lesbian Christians truthfully testifying about their lived reality.

FURTHER READING

Tanya Erzen. *Straight to Jesus: Sexual and Christian Conversions in the Ex-Gay Movement* (Berkeley: University of California Press, 2006). Authored by a sociologist, this is an accurate, well-written study of the ex-gay movement from the 1970s up to about 2005. A must-read for anyone who wants to understand this movement.

Wesley Hill. *Spiritual Friendship: Finding Love in the Church as a Celibate Gay Christian.* Grand Rapids: Brazos, 2015.

Justin Lee. *Torn: Rescuing the Gospel from the Gays-vs.-Christians Debate.* New York: Jericho Books, 2012.

2

Same-Sex Relations in Ancient
Jewish and Christian Thought

Having looked at how the church has responded to gay and lesbian people, we can begin exploring Scripture. What does the Bible say about same-sex relationships? The first crucial step to answering that question is to look at the context of the biblical authors. What did *they* think about same-sex relations?[1] In the current debate, both traditionalists and progressives can fall into anachronistic interpretations. That is, each side tends to project modern ideas onto the Bible that are foreign to the biblical authors themselves. As a result, our interpretations are those of our own imagination rather than reflective of the authors' divinely inspired meaning. As Old Testament scholar Marc Brettler puts it, we must first read Scripture like an Israelite (or an ancient Jew or Christian).[2] Once we understand what the biblical authors believed about sexuality, then we can determine our reasons for retaining, discarding, or expanding on those beliefs.

Same-Sex Relations in Ancient Jewish and Christian Thought

Same-sex relations are rarely mentioned in ancient Near Eastern texts, including the Old Testament. Middle Assyrian Laws

(c. 1076 BCE) condemn same-sex rape and punish false accusations of same-sex intercourse (MALA 19–20). However, several ancient Near Eastern law codes are silent on the matter. Little evidence is available to determine whether same-sex activity was generally rejected or accepted at least until the Greek period, when pederasty was tolerated. Notably, almost all references pertain to males. Perhaps the earliest undisputed reference to females is from Plato's *Symposium* in the fourth century BCE. (Seventh-century poet Sappho is sometimes credited with the earliest reference, but the evidence is ambiguous.)

In the Old Testament, we find two legal citations on same-sex activity; both prohibit male-male sexual intercourse on penalty of death (Lev. 18:22; 20:13). Possibly a few verses refer to male-male ritual prostitution at temples serving foreign gods (e.g., Deut. 23:17–18), but the existence of religious prostitution in the ancient Near East and Israel has been debated in recent scholarship.[3] In any case, the Old Testament authors speak only negatively of same-sex relations. The writers do not provide an explicit reason for this, but if their wording is any indication ("lying with a man as with a woman"), the concern included transgression of gender expectations.

Discussion of same-sex activity increases in the Greco-Roman period. Again, most references are to males, especially to pederasty, for which our earliest evidence is from Crete in the eighth century BCE.[4] Men had sex with boys approximately twelve to seventeen years old. The age differential was not unusual; in that culture, girls commonly were married in their teens to much older men. Among Greeks, pederasty often had a pedagogical component and was not a permanent relationship. Roman law was more restrictive than Greek statutes, prohibiting pederasty with freeborn boys.[5] Only the older, more powerful active partner was expected to achieve sexual gratification. Consensual peer relationships are rarely mentioned.

Homoeroticism during the Greco-Roman period consisted primarily of pederasty. When first-century Jewish writers Philo and Josephus spoke against male-male sexual relations, they typically addressed men having sex with boys.[6] Consensual relationships between adult men were considered offensive because a grown man who took the passive role lost his masculinity in the eyes of Greco-Roman culture. Boys, on the other hand, were not yet men. When they did reach adulthood, they were no longer considered appropriate objects of sexual gratification. The exception to age limits was made with men of lower status (e.g., slaves, prostitutes) or, in the case of the Romans, noncitizens. Such adult slaves, prostitutes, and noncitizens no doubt carried the stigma of being "feminized."

Some Greco-Roman writers condemned same-sex activity for violating gender norms (taking a female role) or showing a perceived excess passion. Some also objected to the lack of procreative potential. The Pythagoreans, Plato, and Musonius Rufus were among those who believed sexual desire should be ordered toward procreation.[7]

In the New Testament, all mention of same-sex relations is negative. Most of these references provide minimal details about the nature of the activity and appear only in vice lists (1 Cor. 6:9–10; 1 Tim. 1:9–10). The apostle Paul likely had in mind the behavior he saw around him, namely, pederasty or sex with male slaves and prostitutes. Of all New Testament texts, Romans 1 provides the most information for analysis and remains *the* text in the church's debate on same-sex relations. We'll look at this text in greater depth in the following chapter.

Why Did the Biblical Authors Condemn Same-Sex Relations?

I have given a brief overview of the historical context because we cannot understand why the biblical authors rejected same-sex relations without attending to the world they lived in. Significantly, there is much agreement between traditionalists and progressives on reasons for the prohibition.

In the Old Testament, the concern centered on these matters:

- violation of gender norms (i.e., a man acting [or lying with a male] like a woman; Lev. 18:22; 20:13)
- lack of procreative potential (more on this below)
- participation in an alleged pagan practice (e.g., Lev. 18:3, 24, 30; 20:23)[8]
- participation in common or religious male prostitution (but evidence for this is questionable; arguments for the existence of religious male prostitution are often based on Deut. 23:17–18, yet the Hebrew terminology in these verses is not entirely clear)

In the New Testament, the concern centered on these matters:[9]

- violation of gender norms (i.e., a man acting like a woman; Paul's use of "unnatural" in Rom.1:26–27; more on this in the next chapter)
- lack of procreative potential (see below)
- participation in a pagan practice (Jewish writings at the time of Paul indicate the belief that homoeroticism was a foreign problem)
- unrestrained or excessive lust (this concern was commonly expressed in ancient writings; so also Paul refers to male sexual partners being "inflamed" with passion in Rom. 1:27)
- participation in common male prostitution and possibly religious male prostitution (but evidence is scant for the latter; New Testament vice lists probably refer to sex with common prostitutes, slaves, or boys; see 1 Cor. 6:9–10; 1 Tim. 1:9–10)

If traditionalists and progressives agree that the biblical authors condemned male same-sex relations (and possibly female; more below), then why the debate? Doesn't that mean the Bible says same-sex relationships are wrong? Not necessarily. Part of the debate is whether the *reasons* the biblical authors give for rejecting homoeroticism are universal. For example, even traditionalists recognize that some rules in the Bible are culturally specific, such as women wearing head coverings. Today, we might not apply this rule because the meaning of "head coverings" doesn't necessarily translate from their culture to ours. Or sometimes a rule was intended for a specific audience, as it was when the writer of Leviticus instructed priests about how to do their job.

Another possibility is that the biblical authors do not specifically address peer same-sex relationships as an ethical issue. (Peer relationships were rare.) Or if the authors do address consensual relations, their objection pertains to practical matters like procreation. Progressives argue that the biblical authors condemned a form of homoeroticism that involved exploitation and misogynistic gender norms. But the biblical authors don't write about the morality of consensual same-sex relationships as we know them today. To put it simply, to say that the biblical authors object to prostitution or pederasty is not to say that the authors object to monogamous, covenanted relationships. That would be comparing apples and oranges.

Traditionalists are willing to concede on some of these points, including recognizing that same-sex relations in antiquity manifested almost exclusively as pederasty and other exploitative practices. Traditionalists also admit that most people are not attracted to the same sex because of unrestrained lust. (Many celibate Christians have testified to same-sex attraction that has nothing to do with excess passion.) Some traditionalists also agree that objection to male-male relations on the grounds of violating gender norms is rooted in outdated views of women as inferior. However, traditionalists are not persuaded by these reasons alone, because the Bible also presents marriage as a union of male and female. The biblical authors appear to be concerned not only with exploitation, excessive lust, and patriarchal customs but also with physical complementarity. Thus, the current debate on same-sex relationships centers on anatomical (or bodily) complementarity, including the role of procreation.

Procreation and Same-Sex Relations

In the next chapter, I will focus exclusively on the arguments surrounding complementarity, as that is the heart of the matter. But first it will be helpful to provide some historical context related to that discussion, specifically regarding procreation.

Scholars agree that the Old Testament authors highly valued procreation. This was common across the ancient Near East because children were essential to economic survival. Genesis 1 highlights reproduction, as do Deuteronomic blessings and curses for obedience or disobedience to God (Gen. 1:11–12, 21–22, 24–25, 28; Deut. 28:4, 11, 18, 41, 51, 53, 56–57, 63). Concern for what happens to semen is also evident (e.g., Gen. 38:8–10). This is likely why Israelite men are prohibited from same-sex relations, but women are not. Procreative potential was thought to reside in male ejaculation.

The New Testament authors continue to esteem progeny (e.g., John 16:21; Eph. 6:1–4; Col. 3:20; 1 Tim. 2:15), but the emphasis is not as strong. In fact, Jesus and Paul downplay marriage (and therefore procreation) while elevating celibacy. However, what is minimized is marriage itself. No evidence exists that Jesus or Paul minimized procreation *within* marriage, which was impossible to prevent without modern contraception. There is little reason to believe that, when it came to those who chose marriage over celibacy, procreation was not envisioned to be an essential component of that. Jewish and Greco-Roman writings commonly connected sex with procreation. This is not to say that Jesus or Paul went to an extreme and valued sex *only* for procreation, but their views are not likely to have been divorced from typical Jewish perspectives on the place of children within marriage.[10]

The connection between procreation and the prohibition against same-sex intercourse is important for our current debate. It raises the question of whether procreation should be required for marriage today. Philo, writing near the time of Paul, argued against same-sex relations because they are not procreative:

Not only in their mad lust for women did they violate
the marriages of their neighbors, but also men mounted
males without respect for the sex nature which the active
partner shares with the passive; and so when they tried
to beget children they were discovered to be incapable
of any but a sterile seed. . . . Certainly, had Greeks and
barbarians joined together in affecting such unions, city
after city would have become a desert, as though depopu-
lated by a pestilential sickness. But God . . . gave increase
in the greatest possible degree to the unions which men
and women naturally make for begetting children, but
abominated and extinguished this unnatural and forbidden intercourse.[11]

Similarly, Josephus writes: "But then, what are our laws about marriage? That law owns no other mixture of sexes but that which nature has appointed, of a man with his wife: and that this be used
only for the procreation of children. But it abhors the mixture of a
male with a male. And if any one do that, death is his punishment."[12]

Paul doesn't name procreation specifically in Romans 1, but like
his contemporaries, he probably has it in mind when he refers to
what is "natural" (*physikēn*) versus "unnatural" (*para physin*).

Concern for procreation could explain, in part, why virtually all
references to same-sex relations in the Bible pertain to men. From
the biblical authors' perspective, men's semen is the essential ele-
ment of procreation. Women are passive receptacles whose wombs
might be open or closed to this seed. Old Testament sex laws do not
prohibit female same-sex activity because, for the Israelite authors,
sex requires penile penetration and ejaculation. Israelite women are,
however, prohibited from having sex with animals, a bizarre act, but
one that hypothetically allows for penetration (Lev. 18:23; 20:16).

This reasoning is also evident in early rabbinic writing. The Bab-
ylonian Talmud records a rabbinic argument concluding that female
same-sex relations, though obscene, do not count as real sex. Thus, a

priest is allowed to marry a woman who has engaged in such activity (*Yevamot* 76a) because she is still considered a virgin. (According to Levitical law, priests are only allowed to marry virgins; Lev. 21:13–15.) Male same-sex relations were far more troublesome to both the biblical authors and the later rabbis than female same-sex relations.

The only possible reference to female same-sex activity in the Bible is Romans 1. However, the text does not specify with whom women exchanged the natural for the unnatural. The theologian Augustine (354–430 CE) speculated that women were having anal sex with men.[13] Thus, when Romans 1:27 says the men did "likewise," the biblical author intends to make a connection to sodomy with women. If this interpretation is accepted, the concern might have been that anal sex was used to prevent pregnancy, thereby enabling promiscuity. In other words, men were wasting their seed and women willingly participated.[14]

Summing It Up

Any discussion on the morality of same-sex relationships today best starts with an examination of the biblical authors' views on sexuality in their historical context. In ancient Near Eastern texts, including the Old Testament, same-sex relations are rarely mentioned. However, the Israelites condemned both participants in male-male sexual intercourse (whether active or passive). Some scholars suggest this condemnation was related to religious male prostitution, but the prevalence of religious prostitution in the ancient Near East and Israel has been challenged in recent scholarship. In the Greco-Roman world, same-sex relations primarily manifested as pederasty, as well as prostitution and sex with slaves. Common Greco-Roman and Jewish reasons for rejecting same-sex activity included lack of procreative potential, violation of gender norms, and perceptions of unrestrained lust. Paul rejected same-sex intercourse within this cultural context.

Today, the debate largely hinges on gender and anatomical complementarity, including the role of procreation. Questions currently being asked are these: Should procreation still be considered a required expectation for sex and marriage? How should we understand gender and anatomical complementarity in terms of morality? These are among the questions I will explore in greater depth in the next chapter.

FURTHER READING

Bernadette J. Brooten. *Love Between Women: Early Christian Responses to Female Homoeroticism.* Chicago: University of Chicago Press, 1996.

Thomas K. Hubbard, ed. *Homosexuality in Greece and Rome: A Sourcebook of Basic Documents.* Berkeley: University of California Press, 2003.

William Loader. "Homosexuality and the Bible." In *Two Views on Homosexuality, the Bible, and the Church*, ed. Preston Sprinkle, 17–48. Grand Rapids: Zondervan, 2016. Loader is a top scholar on the subject of sexuality in ancient Jewish and Christian thought. Look for several of his other books.

Martti Nissinen. *Homoeroticism in the Biblical World: A Historical Perspective.* Minneapolis: Augsburg Fortress, 1998.

Robin Scroggs. *The New Testament and Homosexuality: Contextual Background for Contemporary Debate.* Philadelphia: Fortress, 1983.

3

Key Arguments in Today's Debate on Same-Sex Relationships

Recently I attended a public meeting at a church whose denomination is debating the morality of same-sex relationships. Two high-level officials in the denomination were invited to give a presentation on the topic. I was curious to know how they would handle the issue. I was glad to see they addressed it with grace and respect, but was dismayed by the simplistic and outdated information they provided. In their presentation they summarized six Bible passages commonly cited as proof texts for prohibiting same-sex relationships.[1] The same content could have been heard thirty or forty years ago. These six texts are not the sticking point of the current debate. As I indicated in the previous chapter, traditionalists and progressives largely agree on why the biblical authors condemned same-sex intercourse (at least for men). The crux of the current debate is gender and anatomical complementarity. Accordingly, in this chapter I present key arguments on this pivotal question, beginning with the traditionalist point of view, followed by the progressive perspective. The primary texts for this discussion are Genesis 1–3, Matthew 19:1–6, Mark 10:1–9, Romans 1, Ephesians 5:22–32, and Revelation 19:7–9.

Key Traditionalist Arguments on Same-Sex Relationships

*1. Heterosexual marriage is a creation ordinance
and, therefore, not culturally relative.*

The key traditionalist argument is built on an overarching under-standing of marriage. In the canonical reading (interpretation of the whole of Scripture in its final form), various texts are pulled together to paint an integrated portrait of God's design for marriage. The Genesis creation narratives are essential to this view. In the beginning, God created humankind, "male and female, he created them" (1:27). God had a purpose in designing two sexes, includ-ing the unique capacity to procreate and bring human life into the world. Male and female are intentionally differentiated. The woman is like the man ("flesh of my flesh"), but also different because she has been separated out of man. The Hebrew word *kenegdo* captures this distinction: Eve is set before Adam as his counterpart. This reading is reinforced by other pairings in Genesis 1, including light/darkness, earth/sky, sun/moon, and land/sea. Thus, given sexual differentia-tion and its procreative gift, a man "leaves his father and mother and is united to his wife" (2:24). Marriage is inscribed in creation itself as a union between male and female. Same-sex relationships are a violation of God's purposeful design for sexuality.

The New Testament supports this view. When explaining why people should remain married and not divorce, Jesus argues, "Haven't you read . . . that at the beginning the Creator 'made them male and fe-male,' and said, 'For this reason a man will leave his father and mother and be united to his wife, and the two will become one flesh'? So they are no longer two, but one flesh. Therefore what God has joined to-gether, let no one separate" (Matt. 19:4–6; see also Mark 10:1–9). Je-sus is addressing a question about divorce, but in the process clarifies God's will for those "joined together." He quotes two texts: Genesis 1:27 and 2:24. Even if these beginning chapters of Genesis derive from different ancient sources (as most scholars believe), Jesus reads them together as a unified text. Thus, we should follow his interpretive approach. Moreover, Jesus could have made his argument using only 2:24 (one flesh), but chose to include the additional comment about male and female.

2. Marriage is ordered toward procreation, but procreation is not required to validate a marriage.

As Genesis indicates, God made male and female and commanded them to multiply and fill the earth. Thus all marriage should be open to and ordered toward procreation. Our bodies tell us that male and female are sexually complementary. Sperm is produced and delivered via the male sexual organs (testes and penis). The vagina receives sperm and channels it toward fertilization of an egg. Male and female sex organs don't fully make sense apart from each other. Their reproductive functions are contingent on one another. To pretend that our bodies say *nothing* about God's (or even biology's) design for sex fails to honestly engage what we know about male and female physicality.

This attention to bodily complementarity is also why traditionalists bless infertile couples to marry even if they cannot procreate. The creation design is not merely procreation itself but also the anatomical complementarity that leads to that result. Infertile heterosexual couples can still use their bodies sexually in the intended complementary way. They can become "one flesh," as Genesis describes. Infertile couples can also still participate in gender complementarity, which for some traditionalists is grounded in certain understandings of male and female roles (e.g., a wife's submission to her husband). As the creation narrative states, woman was created to be "a helper" for the man (Gen. 2:18). However, gender complementarity can also be understood in an egalitarian sense as basic differences between men and women beyond sex and reproduction. Such distinctions can be controversial and are not easily defined, but traditionalists point out that even social scientific studies demonstrate that men and women have differences.[2]

3. Same-sex desire is the result of the fall.

According to Genesis 3, disobedience to God led to a fallen, disordered world. Our sexuality is affected by this and needs to be redeemed. In Romans 1, Paul casts same-sex desire in the context of this fall. Romans 1 has Genesis as a backdrop. Allusions can be seen in the phrases "creation of the world" and "the Creator" (Rom. 1:20, 25), as well as in the distinct terms "males" (*arsenes*) and "females" (*thēleiai*) in verses 26–27 per the Greek translation of Genesis 1:27 (instead of "men" [*andres*] and "women" [*gynaikes*]).[3] Romans 1 also has echoes of the Greek translation of Genesis related to images and animals. For example, see the vocabulary in common:

> Then God said, "Let us make humankind [*anthropos*] in our image [*eikon*], after our likeness [*homoiosis*], so they may rule over the fish of the sea, and the birds [*peteina*] of the air, over the cattle, and over all the earth, and over all the creatures that move on the earth [*herpeta*]." (Gen. 1:26 NET)

> [They] exchanged the glory of the immortal God for images [*eikon*] made to look like [*homoioma*] a mortal human being [*anthropos*] and birds [*peteina*] and animals and reptiles [*herpeta*]. (Rom. 1:23)

Moreover, Jewish writers around the time of Paul, including Philo and Josephus, as well as some Greco-Roman writers, referred to "natural" (*physikos* or *kata physin*) and "unnatural" (*para physin*) in the context of procreation, which requires anatomical complementarity. Paul does not specifically mention procreation in Romans 1, but there is no reason to believe that his use of *para physin* is completely divorced from the way it was understood by other Jewish and Greco-Roman writers who made an explicit connection between the phrase and procreation. This view is supported by Paul's allusions to Genesis.

Since Romans 1 denounces same-sex intercourse on the basis of God's intentional creation of male and female, the prohibition cannot be reduced to only exploitative relationships characteristic of pederasty, prostitution, or master and slave. Also, the inclusion of women as guilty of unnatural intercourse indicates that all forms of same-sex relations are in view, since female-female relationships did not manifest in the same way as male-male relationships in antiquity.

4. Heterosexual marriage is a living icon or symbol of the union between Christ and the church.

Marriage is meant to be a living icon of the beautiful relationship between God and humankind, as well as the relationship within the Trinity itself. Marriage between a man and a woman is a symbol that witnesses to divine realities.

The Bible starts and ends with marriage. At creation, Adam and Eve are brought together in a complementary union (Gen. 1–2). At the end of time, Christ, the groom, is united with his bride, the church (Rev. 19:7–9).[4] In Ephesians 5 Paul drives home this connection of marriage between man and woman and marriage between Christ and the church: "Husbands, love your wives, just as Christ loved the church and gave himself up for her. . . . After all, no one ever hated their own body, but they feed and care for their body, just as Christ does the church—for we are members of his body. 'For this reason a man will leave his father and mother and be united to his wife, and the two will become one flesh.' This is a profound mystery—but I am talking about Christ and the church" (vv. 25, 29–32).

The metaphor makes sense only if differentiation is present. Christ, who is God, is united with human beings. Same-sex marriage would be akin to saying Christ married Christ or the church married the church. Same-sex relationships do not reflect essential "otherness" and, thus, cannot serve as living symbols of Christ and the church.

Key Progressive Arguments on Same-Sex Relationships

1. Covenant fidelity, not sexual differentiation, is the foundation of biblical marriage.

Progressives agree that male and female are part of God's good creation, but they believe loyal, covenanted love, not sexual differentiation, is the foundation of biblical marriage. Genesis 2 is a key text, as well as Jesus's interpretations of Genesis in Mark 10. Genesis 2:18 reads, "It is not good for the human being [ha'adam] to be alone; I will make for him a strong ally [ezer] as his counterpart" (my translation).[5] God makes this observation about Adam when the first man is not literally alone. God is there, talking to him about the trees and urging him to eat abundantly (vv. 16–18). God is good company for the man, but the Creator also recognizes and takes no offense that Adam needs someone else too (vv. 16–18). God is not deemed an appropriate counterpart. The same is true for the animals. Adam inspects all the creatures but doesn't call any of them ally or counterpart (v. 20). A turning point comes when God creates woman directly from Adam's body. The man wakes up and immediately exclaims, "This is now bone of my bones and flesh of my flesh!" (v. 23).[6] He delights in her similarity to him.

Eve is from the man's very own body. Adam proclaims that she is the same as him. Unlike the animals, the woman is kin. That which is "other" (God and the animals) is deemed insufficient to be Adam's counterpart. When Adam marvels that Eve is "flesh of my

30

flesh," he announces a kinship bond. This kinship language appears elsewhere in the Bible. Laban tells Jacob, "Surely you are my bone and my flesh!" (Gen. 29:14).[7] The story of Adam and Eve demonstrates that marriage is, first of all, a union founded on commonality, not differentiation.

Jesus's interpretation of the creation narratives adds additional insight (Mark 10:2–12). He quotes Genesis 1:27 and 2:24 to argue that marriage is a permanent bond. Divorce obscures the very foundation of marriage, which is covenant. Traditionalists argue that Jesus's reference to "male and female" (Mark 10:6) is evidence that he is making a statement about sexual differentiation. But good exegesis requires us to ask *why* Jesus refers to male and female. Clearly, it's not because the Pharisees have a question about sexual differentiation. For them, male and female are a given. Their question is "Can a man lawfully divorce his wife?" Attending to their topic of concern helps us understand Jesus's reference to Genesis. Namely, the Pharisees use the law of Moses to argue their case (v. 4), and Jesus appeals to an earlier precedent to refute them.

Jesus commonly quoted short phrases from Old Testament texts. These phrases would remind his audiences of the broader scriptural context of the quotation. Thus, when Jesus refers to male and female, he is using shorthand. The context of Jesus's quote is Genesis 1:27: "Then God said, 'Let us make humankind in our image, after our likeness.' . . . God created humankind in his own image, in the image of God he created them; male and female he created them" (vv. 26–27 NET). Jesus refers to male and female to establish an earlier precedent for marital standards than the Mosaic law, which the Pharisees are using to make their case. In other words, Moses's law on divorce is inferior to the Genesis account from which Jesus builds his argument.

Jesus reads Genesis 1:27 as God creating human beings as a pair, but his argument does not focus on sexual differentiation. Instead, he stresses the unity of two people. He quotes Genesis 2:24, saying that when a man leaves his family of origin and is joined to his wife, "the two will become one flesh" (Mark 10:8). He intensifies the point by repeating this again: "So they are no longer two, but one flesh" (v. 8). The two are joined together as one. Jesus drives home his argument: "Therefore what God has joined together, let no one separate" (v. 9). The crux of the argument is about keeping two people together. Jesus is expounding a case for the permanence of marriage, not for male-female marriage, which the Pharisees would not have questioned.

This reading is confirmed by the version of Genesis that Jesus quotes. The word "two" does not appear in the Masoretic (Hebrew) Text of Genesis 2:24. Jesus is quoting the Greek version (or the author of Mark puts the Greek version in Jesus's mouth). Given that manuscripts without the word "two" were in circulation, Jesus's use of the Greek version appears to be intentional.[8] Some scholars believe "two" is a later gloss added to the Greek translation of the Old Testament (the Septuagint) because the Jewish translators wanted to reject polygamy.[9] Thus, Jesus implies that divorce is a problem because it leads to having more than one spouse (Mark 10:11–12). In essence, Jesus reinforces that, from the beginning of creation, God intended marriage to be a unity of two. That oneness should never be ruptured or shared with other spouses through remarriage after divorce. Marriage is defined by fidelity.

To recap the preceding discussion, we find the following key aspects of marriage in Genesis 2 and Jesus's interpretation of Genesis:[10]

- companionship (not good to be alone)
- mutual support of a strong ally (*ezer*; not unilateral since Adam is by definition a counterpart [*kenegdo*]; as counterparts they mirror each other)
- commonality and similarity
- human spouse (bestiality ruled out; animals are too "other")
- establishment of "flesh of my flesh" kinship tie (no incest because it's redundant; one does not need to form a kinship bond

with someone who is already kin; one must leave family of
origin to find a spouse [Gen. 2:24])
- faithfulness (no adultery or divorce)
- a pair (no polygamous relationships)

Traditionalists sometimes argue that sexual differentiation is required for marriage in order to prevent a slippery slope into immorality. If we allow gay people to marry, then everyone will want to marry
their pets, siblings, and half the college class. But differentiation is not
the basis for protection against these things. Israel's own history is a
testimony to that. Polygamy was not rejected by the biblical authors
until the Greco-Roman period after the Greeks introduced monogamy to the ancient Near East. Scripture gives other reasons besides
sexual differentiation (as listed above) to explain why people should
not engage in polygamy, incest, bestiality, adultery, and divorce.

Progressives acknowledge that Genesis 1 includes procreation,
which requires sexual differentiation, but they point out that the
biblical authors don't define marriage by procreation. Lack of children does not annul the bond. For example, Elkanah reassures his
wife, Hannah, that their marriage is valuable despite her barrenness
(1 Sam. 1:8). One can have a marriage without children, but one cannot have marriage without fidelity. Faithfulness is the cornerstone of
biblical marriage and is exemplified by the nuptial metaphor in the
Bible: God's marriage to Israel is used expressly to illustrate covenant loyalty or lack of it.

2. Procreation is minimized in the New Testament.

In Genesis 1, procreation is the primary purpose of sexual differentiation. But in the New Testament procreation is explicitly minimized.
This has implications for defining marriage.

The Old Testament authors highly esteemed fertility. One reason for this is that the Israelites did not have a developed theology

of immortality or resurrection. A man's legacy lived on through his offspring. His name and inheritance were passed down from generation to generation, keeping his presence alive in the memories of his descendants. In the Greco-Roman period, Jews began to discuss the afterlife in greater depth. By the first century, resurrection was a key theological concept for Jews (except the Sadducees). Significantly, with immortality came the possibility of a man living on apart from his offspring.

Jesus reflects this developing theology when he says, "The people of this age marry and are given in marriage. But those who are considered worthy of taking part in the age to come and in the resurrection from the dead will neither marry nor be given in marriage, and they can no longer die; for they are like the angels. They are God's children, since they are children of the resurrection" (Luke 20:34–36).[11] The reason for no marriage at the end of the age is that people will not die. In other words, marriage, which currently perpetuates life through procreation, will not be necessary. Immortality will perpetuate life. Jesus's death and resurrection make eternal life possible. That is why, from Christianity's earliest stages, celibacy has been a prominent way to live into this eschatological reality.

If procreation's purpose of passing down one's name and legacy is overtaken by immortality, this has implications for marriage. Some critics might counter this by saying that Jesus and Paul did not diminish the role of procreation *within* marriage. They championed celibacy, not childless marriages. True, but that was by necessity. In the first century, lack of reliable contraception meant that singleness was the only confident way to avoid procreation. Modern contraception offers new possibilities for modeling the hope of immortality in non-procreative marriages alongside celibacy. The value of such marriages is greater freedom for couples to engage in kingdom work while still benefiting from mutual support.

Granted, some traditionalists object to contraception. The Catholic Church as a whole, as well as certain Protestant groups (e.g., Quiverfull), maintain that sexual acts should be ordered toward conceiving a child. They believe procreation is essential to the definition of marriage. Even so, the church has consistently made exceptions for infertile couples. The Catholic Church states in its *Canon Code of Law*, "Sterility neither prohibits nor nullifies marriage" (1084.3). Protestants also regularly affirm marriage for infertile couples. Thus, couples that cannot procreate *are* permitted to marry.

Procreative potential is often cited as a reason to exclude same-sex relationships, but the exception for infertile couples reveals that anatomical complementarity—the fittedness of the penis and the vagina—is the primary issue. For this reason the Catholic Church prohibits impotent people from getting married (*Canon* 1084.1). That means if a young man goes off to war and sustains injury to his genitals, preventing insertion into the vagina, he is forbidden from marrying his sweetheart back home.[12] The Catholic Church requires him to remain single for the rest of his life. The inability to perform that one specific act means he is forced to give up all the companionship and experiences of lifelong covenant he could have had with the person he loves most. Thus, the fixation on anatomical complementarity for marriage causes unnecessary suffering not only for gay and lesbian people but also for straight people who have injuries or other conditions affecting penis-vagina intercourse.[13]

In essence, Genesis 1 indicates procreation is the reason for sexual differentiation. But the New Testament minimizes procreation because of the confidence of eternal life. This has implications for non-procreative marriages, including same-sex unions.

3. Paul's use of "unnatural" (para physin) in Romans 1 must be understood in his historical context.

Paul did not use the phrase "unnatural" (*para physin*; contrary to nature) in a novel way, divorced from his context. As discussed in Chapter 2, both Jewish and Greco-Roman writers often used this term in reference to non-procreative sex and patriarchal gender norms. The de-emphasis on procreation in the New Testament does not contradict this objection to non-procreative sex. Paul advocated celibacy, not marital sex devoid of natural consequences. Without technological advancements in contraception, he could not imagine regular sexual relations between a husband and a wife which didn't result in procreation (except that of infertile couples). Thus, it's reasonable to conclude that when Paul refers to *para physin*, his concern includes the non-procreative nature of same-sex acts.

Paul's use of *para physin* is best understood in light of first-century Stoicism, a philosophy that influenced his thinking. Behavior contrary to nature was understood to be anything that "places humans out of sync with both the cosmos as a whole and with the deepest and truest aspects of themselves as persons."[14] In other words, Paul believed that every human being is heterosexual and that to achieve a rightly ordered self a person must conform to heterosexual desire and behavior. If Paul knew about medical theories for sexual orientation, he likely rejected them, as did his near contemporary Philo. (Philo dismissed Plato's theory of innate etiology for same-sex attraction as absurd.[15]) Paul never addresses the reality that gay people who attempt to make themselves "rightly ordered" heterosexuals actually experience tremendous discordance.[16] Not only is it impossible for most, but often such attempts to become straight lead to despair and greater internal disorder.

4. Romans 1 does not describe most gay and lesbian people.

In Romans 1, Paul does not address ordinary gay or lesbian people. His exposure to same-sex relations is primarily through unbelievers. Like other Jewish writers of his time, he believed same-sex relations were a pagan problem caused by rejecting God. Paul describes those with same-sex desire as heathens who have been given over to consuming lust as punishment from God (1:26–27).

Traditionalists argue that Paul has the fall in mind and means to include all humanity in this graphic depiction of pagans. As evidence, they cite perceived parallels with Genesis 1. However, these alleged connections—general imagery (animals) and terms ("Creator")—also appear at other points in the Bible.[17] Nowhere in Romans 1 does Paul mention Adam. Nor is there any reference to Genesis 3 and the infamous disobedience. Instead of Genesis, Paul makes his argument in conversation with Wisdom of Solomon. For comparison, note the similarities between Romans 1 and Wisdom 13 and 14:

> Romans 1:19–20: "[W]hat may be known about God is plain to them, because God has made it plain to them. For since the creation of the world God's invisible qualities— his eternal power and divine nature—have been clearly seen, being understood from what has been made, so that people are without excuse."

> Wisdom 13:7–9 RSV: "For as they live among [God's] works they keep searching, and they trust in what they see, because the things that are seen are beautiful. Yet again, not even they are to be excused; for if they had the power to know so much that they could investigate the world, how did they fail to find sooner the Lord of these things?"

> Romans 1:21–22: "For although they knew God, they neither glorified him as God nor gave thanks to him, but their thinking became futile and their foolish hearts were darkened. Although they claimed to be wise, they became fools."

> Wisdom 13:1 RSV: "For all men who were ignorant of God were foolish by nature; and they were unable from the

good things that are seen to know him who exists, nor
did they recognize the craftsman while paying heed to
his works."

Romans 1:23: "[They] exchanged the glory of the immortal
God for images made to look like a mortal human being
and birds and animals and reptiles."

Wisdom 13:10 RSV: "But miserable . . . are the men who
give the name 'gods' to the works of men's hands, gold
and silver fashioned with skill, and likenesses of animals."

The similarities between Romans and Wisdom are more exten-
sive than what I have listed here, including a vice list of immorality
that cites sexual sin (compare Rom. 1:24–32 with Wis. 14:23–27).
This connection has long been recognized by scholars.[18] It's beyond
the scope of this chapter to provide an in-depth comparison of the
books. The point is that Genesis is not the backdrop for Paul; Wisdom of Solomon is the text he is engaging. That has crucial implications for understanding the meaning of Romans 1.

Paul doesn't use Wisdom merely to copy it. In fact, he over-
turns the position of Wisdom that gives Israel greater favor before
God than the pagans.[19] Employing a rhetorical strategy, Paul insists
that everyone is equally subject to God's judgment (Rom. 2:1). The
point of Romans 1 and 2 is that *God shows no partiality* (2:11). These
two chapters do not describe a fall that infects all humanity with a
sinful nature. Nor is Paul making a claim here that the pagans represent all fallen humanity. Paul eventually develops his argument of
sin in later chapters of Romans, but at this point he is focused on
impartiality and divine justice.

Instead of inborn fallen natures, Paul describes adult pagans
whose thinking *became* "futile" after they *knowingly* rejected God
(Rom. 1:21). He portrays this futility of mind as the cause of same-sex
desire and behavior. This description of pagans intentionally defying

God does not reflect the reality of most gay and lesbian people, and certainly not those who are Christian. The church has historically interpreted Romans 1 as saying gay people are heathens. Only recently has this passage been reframed to include Christians who happen to struggle with same-sex attraction.[20] But that is clearly not the imagery depicted. In essence, Paul does not address the question of gay people who love God and want to share their life with someone in a caring, monogamous relationship.

5. Same-sex relationships can symbolize the union between Christ and the church.

In Ephesians 5:25–32, Paul uses marriage as a metaphor for Christ's relationship with the church. We find this same metaphorical use in the Old Testament where God is pictured as Israel's spouse. Traditionalists argue that only male and female can model this image of Christ and the church. Sexual differentiation is required to represent the "otherness" of the divine-human union. Allegedly, male and female are defined by how they are different and "other" from one another, making them suitable for imaging the marriage of God to human beings. Traditionalists believe that such differentiation is essential to representing the image of Christ and the church, and therefore marriage must be between male and female.

The theology of marriage as "otherness" was popularized by theologians Karl Barth and Hans Urs von Balthasar (who was influenced by Barth).[21] Both focus on sexual differentiation between men and women as representing the relationship between Christ and the church. They understood differentiation within traditional gender roles (man as the leader and woman as the one who submits). Thus, gender and sexual differentiation get tangled up in their theology of the Godhead. There are significant theological problems with connecting gender and the Godhead in this way. (See the sources at the end of the reading list below.) The most obvious is that this reading fails to acknowledge what Paul actually says. Nothing in Ephesians 5 requires or even suggests this emphasis on otherness.

Paul emphasizes similarity, not difference. In this way, Ephesians is similar to Genesis 2. As previously discussed, Genesis describes Adam's need for someone *similar* to himself. God and the animals are too "other" to be suitable partners. When Adam sees Eve, he exclaims, "Flesh of my flesh, bone of my bone!" This connotation is evident in Ephesians. Paul says a husband is to love his wife *as his own body*, which highlights similarity, not difference (Eph. 5:28).[22] Christ and the church are metaphorically imaged as *one person*, not differentiated beings. Christ is the head on the shoulders and limbs of the church that is his own body.[23]

As with the marriage metaphor in the Old Testament, the Ephesians metaphor is about faithful love. A husband should give self-sacrificially to his wife (Eph. 5:25), love her as his own body (v. 29), and nourish and care for her with tenderness (v. 29). And echoing Jesus's interpretation of Genesis, Paul says that the "two" shall be united as one (v. 31). This unity of two is what symbolizes Christ and the church. As a *pair*, same-sex couples can also exhibit and witness to divine realities through self-sacrificial love.

Summing It Up

Too often discussions on same-sex relationships rehash the same unhelpful arguments based on six proof texts. But that is not the heart of the debate. Both sides—traditionalist and progressive—agree that the biblical authors opposed same-sex relations, in part, for exploitative reasons. Instead, disagreement centers on gender and anatomical complementarity. Traditionalists believe heterosexual marriage is a permanent ordinance per God's creation of male and female (Gen. 1–3). Therefore, the prohibition against same-sex relations is not merely a product of temporal cultural factors. Traditionalists also argue that Romans 1 refers to the fall and that Paul's reference to "unnatural" includes violation of anatomical complementarity. Finally, traditionalists assert that the marriage between Christ and the church can only be conveyed by the "otherness" of male and female (Eph. 5). In response, progressives argue that Genesis and Jesus's interpretation of Genesis portray loyal, covenanted love, not sexual differentiation, as the primary foundation of marriage. Moreover, procreation—the reason for sexual differentiation—is minimized in the New Testament because of the hope of eternal life. Progressives also assert that Paul does not refer to the fall in Romans 1, which, following Wisdom of Solomon, depicts pagans, not Christians struggling with fallen natures. Finally, progressives point out that Ephesians emphasizes similarity, not otherness, to convey the metaphor of Christ and the church.

FURTHER READING FOR THE TRADITIONALIST VIEW

Kevin DeYoung. *What Does the Bible Really Teach about Homosexuality?*, 1–59 (part 1 only). Wheaton, IL: Crossway, 2015.

Robert Gagnon. *The Bible and Homosexual Practice: Texts and Hermeneutics*. Nashville: Abingdon, 2001. For an abbreviated version of his arguments, see his essay countering Dan Via in Robert A. J. Gagnon and Dan O. Via, *Homosexuality and the Bible: Two Views*. Minneapolis: Fortress, 2003.

Wesley Hill. "Christ, Scripture, and Spiritual Friendship." In *Homosexuality, the Bible, and the Church*, ed. Preston Sprinkle, 124–47. Grand Rapids: Zondervan, 2016.

Christopher C. Roberts. *Creation and Covenant: The Significance of Sexual Difference in the Moral Theology of Marriage*. New York: Bloomsbury Academic, 2008.

Preston Sprinkle. *People to Be Loved: Why Homosexuality Is Not Just an Issue*. Grand Rapids: Zondervan, 2015.

William Webb. *Slaves, Women, and Homosexuals: Exploring the Hermeneutics of Cultural Analysis*. Downers Grove, IL: IVP Academic, 2001.

N. T. Wright. "What Is Marriage For?" *Plough Quarterly* 6 (2015): 38–43.

FURTHER READING FOR THE PROGRESSIVE VIEW

James V. Brownson. *Bible, Gender, Sexuality: Reframing the Church's Debate on Same-Sex Relationships.* Grand Rapids: Eerdmans, 2013.

Deirdre J. Good, Willis J. Jenkins, Cynthia B. Kittred, and Eugene F. Rogers. "A Theology of Marriage including Same-Sex Couples: A View from the Liberals." *Anglican Theological Review* 93 (2011): 51–87.

William Loader. "Homosexuality and the Bible." In *Two Views on Homosexuality, the Bible, and the Church*, ed. Preston Sprinkle, 17–48. Grand Rapids: Zondervan, 2016.

Robert Song. *Covenant and Calling: Towards a Theology of Same-Sex Relationships.* London: SCM, 2014.

Matthew Vines. *God and the Gay Christian: The Biblical Case in Support of Same-Sex Relationships.* New York: Convergent Books, 2014.

See also the two articles below on the problem of superimposing gender on God, which traditionalists tend to do to make a case for sexual differentiation in marriage.

D. Glenn Butner. "Eternal Functional Subordination and the Problem of the Divine Will." *Journal of the Evangelical Theological Society* 58 (2015): 131–49.

Fred Sanders. "You, Me, and the Heavenly Three?" *Christianity Today*, August 8, 2013. http://www.christianitytoday.com/ct/2013/august-web-only/why-trinity-cant-tell-us-about-gender.html.

4

Fifty Shekels for Rape?
Making Sense of Old Testament Laws

In the previous chapter, I summarized key arguments in the debate on same-sex relationships. Traditionalists believe the biblical authors' rejection of same-sex relations is rooted in God's design for creation and therefore not culturally relative. Progressives argue that the cornerstone of biblical marriage is covenant fidelity, not sexual differentiation. This view allows the possibility of same-sex partnerships, even if the biblical authors could not conceptualize that option within the confines of their cultural context. This is where the two sides of the debate tend to stalemate. To help the conversation forward, I focus the rest of this book on additional arguments that are currently being overlooked. In this chapter we will explore Old Testament laws to gain a better grasp of what it means to use the Bible for our own ethical practice. Traditionalists frequently appeal to the Levitical prohibition against male same-sex relations (Lev. 18:22; 20:13). But does this law apply today?

It can be difficult to make sense of Old Testament laws. Not long ago, I received an email from a friend who was reading Deuteronomy: "I'm having trouble with certain verses. Today it's chapter 22 ... fifty shekels for rape, and then the woman has to marry her rapist? Stoning for adultery?" My friend was using a "read the Bible in a year" devotional curriculum and got more than she bargained for! She wasn't sure what to do with these texts. In what sense are they Scripture for Christian life and practice? The texts also raised questions for her about the character of God. Does God think it's okay to require a rape victim to marry her perpetrator?

Understandably, many Christians find it easier to ignore the Old Testament than to make sense of it. But taking a closer look at these texts will help us navigate the debate on same-sex relationships. Traditionalists argue that just as Old Testament laws on incest and adultery are still relevant, so also is the command against same-sex relations. Progressives argue that the prohibition is applicable only to the Israelites and their cultural context. The mandate is no more binding on Christians than the law against eating shrimp (Lev. 11:9–12). Traditionalists counter that we can be sure the Levitical law is still valid because the New Testament reiterates the prohibition.

So, who is right? Both sides offer compelling points, but both fall short of making their case. Progressives are correct that not all the specific laws in the Old Testament are relevant to Christian practice, but they throw out the baby with the bath water. Leviticus *does* contain many relevant concerns for us today, including prohibitions against adultery, incest, and mistreating people with disabilities. Traditionalists are correct that many important laws are reiterated in the New Testament, but they fail to account for relevant commands that are *not* in the New Testament. The law in the Old Testament against bestiality, which appears directly after the reference to same-sex relations, does not show up anywhere in the New Testament. Surely, reiteration (or lack thereof) cannot be the only criterion for how we appropriate ethics from the Bible.

We can begin to make sense of Old Testament law collections, including the Levitical prohibitions, when we grasp the overarching reasons why the biblical authors included them in Scripture. The first confusion to clear up is that *the culture of the ancient Near East (or the Greco-Roman world) is distinct from biblical inspiration itself.* Ancient Near Eastern culture was not divine, even though the biblical message that was articulated from within that culture is divinely inspired. The biblical authors wrote with an accent, so to speak. The language and social structures of that time period influenced how the message was delivered. If God had chosen to inspire the writing of Scripture in our society today, it would have sounded different, using the vocabulary and social structures of twenty-first-century America. We have to get used to the biblical authors' accent to understand what they are saying.

Often readers approach the Bible as if it fell from heaven or is the product of mechanical dictation (given to passive writers in a trance). This results in assuming that the biblical authors' *accent* is divine. But God spoke to the Israelites in their cultural context. Scripture is a collaborative effort between God and human beings. Not surprisingly, the Israelite law collections are similar to those of other nations in the ancient Near East. The law regarding rape victims is a cultural artifact (one that is still being addressed today).[1] In essence, discerning the divine meaning of Scripture requires distinguishing the inspired message from the temporal, cultural mode of delivery. Therefore, to understand the enduring theological significance of the Old Testament laws, we must attend to both the historical-cultural background and the narrative context.

Old Testament Laws in Their Ancient Near Eastern Context

The most significant law collections of the ancient Near East date from approximately 2100 to 700 BCE.[2] They include Ur-Nammu (ca. 2100, Ur), Lipit-Eshtar (ca. 1930, Isin), Eshnunnu (ca. 1770, Eshnunnu), Hammurabi (ca. 1750, Babylon), Hittite (ca. 1650–1500, Anatolia), Middle Assyrian (ca. 1076, Assur), and Neo-Babylonian (ca. 700, Sippar). It's not certain when the biblical law collections were written. Some scholars suggest they were written around the eighth to the sixth century BCE. Possibly older laws were edited over time to their present form. A conservative view places the writing of the law collections earlier, at the time of Moses, around 1250 BCE, but the type of Hebrew we have in the Bible did not exist then. In addition, the Torah (the first five books of the Hebrew Scriptures or Old Testament) shows obvious signs of being written by more than one author. In any case, most of the ancient Near Eastern law collections are older than those found in the Old Testament, and the biblical authors were influenced by these pre-existing laws.

The Old Testament law collections include the Covenant Collection (Exod. 21–23), the Holiness Collection (Lev. 17–26), the Deuteronomic Collection (Deut. 12–26), the Decalogue (Exod. 20:2–17; Deut. 5:6–21), and the Ritual Decalogue (Exod. 34:10–26). There are additional sacrificial and purity laws, especially in Leviticus. The law collections were written in two legal genres: casuistic and apodictic. Casuistic law is case law that is not intended to address every possible legal situation. Instead, a conditional formula is presented and used for drawing conclusions based on association or inference ("*If* a man rents an ox . . ."). Apodictic law is a direct command or prohibition ("You shall not . . ."). Casuistic law was common in other ancient Near Eastern law collections, but the apodictic form less so than in the biblical text. Here is a comparative look.[3]

Case of the Goring Ox

Eshnunnu:
If an ox is a gorer and the ward authorities so notify its owner but he fails to keep his ox in check and it gores a man and thus causes his death, the owner of the ox shall weigh and deliver 40 shekels of silver. (A iv 15–18, B iv 20)

Hammurabi:
If an ox gores to death a man while it is passing through the streets, that case has no basis for a claim. If a man's ox is a known gorer, and the authorities of his city quarter notify him that it is a known gorer, but he does not

blunt[?] its horns or control his ox, and that ox gores to death a member of the *awilu*-class [an upper-class citizen], he [the owner] shall give 30 shekels of silver. (xliv 44–65)

Israelite:
If an ox gores a man or a woman so that either dies, then the ox must surely be stoned and its flesh must not be eaten, but the owner of the ox will be acquitted. But if the ox had the habit of goring, and its owner was warned, and he did not take the necessary precautions, and then it killed a man or a woman, the ox must be stoned and the man must be put to death. If a ransom is set for him, then he must pay the redemption for his life according to whatever amount was set for him. (Exod. 21:28–30 NET)

Case of the Violence-Induced Miscarriage

Lipit-Eshtar:
If [a man] strikes the daughter of a man and causes her to lose her fetus, he shall weigh and deliver 30 shekels of silver. (P rev. iii' 2'-6')

Hammurabi:
If an *awilu* strikes a woman of the *awilu*-class and thereby causes her to miscarry her fetus, he shall weigh and deliver 10 shekels of silver for her fetus. If that woman should die, they shall kill his daughter. (xli 23–34)

Middle Assyrian:
If a man strikes a woman of the *awilu*-class, thereby causing her to abort her fetus and they prove the charges against him and find him guilty—he shall pay 9,000 shek-

els of lead; they shall strike him 50 blows with rods; he shall perform the king's service for one full month. (ii 98–104)

Israelite:
If people are fighting and hit a pregnant woman and she [has a miscarriage][4] but there is no serious injury, the offender must be fined whatever the woman's husband demands and the court allows. But if there is serious injury, you are to take life for life, eye for eye, tooth for tooth, hand for hand, foot for foot, burn for burn, wound for wound, bruise for bruise. (Exod. 21:22–25)

Similarities and Differences

As you can see, both cases (the goring ox and the miscarriage) are casuistic, presenting a conditional scenario with a resolution. They also share the same subject matter. The ancient Near Eastern law collections, including the biblical text, are concerned with general social issues. While they might not agree on how to resolve a case, all the law collections address the following:[5]

- relationships (e.g., marriage, divorce, adoption, legitimate/illegitimate sexual partners)
- property damage (e.g., injury to slaves and animals)
- crime (e.g., murder, theft, false testimony, adultery)
- business transactions (e.g., buying/selling, loans/debts, inheritance, the management of slaves)

The ancient Near Eastern law collections represent a commitment to justice. We might view some of the laws and punishments as primitive or even barbaric; however, the laws are attempts to render fair compensation when someone has been wronged and to promote proper conduct. Some of the ancient Near Eastern law collections have prologues affirming the importance of righteousness and justice. A short excerpt from Hammurabi's prologue reads, "At that time, the gods Anu and Enlil, for the enhancement of the well-being of the people, named me by my name: Hammurapi, the pious prince, who venerates the gods, to make justice prevail in the land, to abolish the wicked and the evil, to prevent the strong from oppressing the weak."[6]

Despite obvious similarities, differences between the biblical law collections and those of other nations are also apparent. Most significantly, the biblical collections are embedded in a broader narrative; the other ancient Near Eastern collections are not. Although the Israelite collections might have existed independently at one time, they have been recontextualized and preserved in Scripture as blended genre (legal text with narrative). The recontextualization of the laws naturally affects their meaning.

A second difference is the source of the laws. The biblical text describes God as giving the statutes through a prophet. Other ancient Near Eastern collections are given by a king who states that the gods have provided him wisdom and authority to make and enforce the laws. Hammurabi gives credit to the gods for choosing him and commanding him to provide justice, but he ultimately refers to the laws as his own pronouncements and judgments. Obeying the king's laws was tantamount to showing allegiance and subservience to him. This is important for understanding the significance of Mount Sinai: *God, not a human king, is the source and enforcer of justice.* Thus, what might have been considered a civil matter is now categorized explicitly as sin against the Creator of the universe.

Although the prologues and epilogues of other ancient Near Eastern law collections show reverence for the gods, the actual laws do not have the religious connotation that the biblical laws have.[7] For example, Deuteronomy 24:14–15 states, "Do not take advantage of a hired worker who is poor and needy. . . . Otherwise they may cry to the LORD against you, and you will be guilty of sin."

In addition to these religious motivational addendums to some of the biblical laws, the narrative context of the law collections provides a theological framework indicating that to act justly is to show allegiance to God and not only a human king. People are accountable not only to human governments but to God, an impartial judge who stands above self-interests and agendas of earthly rulers. For the biblical authors, God is a just God who gives laws out of a desire for human beings to live in a manner congruent with justice.

The Enduring Meaning of Old Testament Laws

So, how might we understand these laws as inspired text, particularly given that older laws from other nations influenced the biblical authors? In what way are they inspired if they are so thoroughly enmeshed in the culture of that time period? One common cause of misinterpretation of Old Testament laws is that we focus more on *what* the laws are than on *why* they are included in Scripture. Inspiration resides not necessarily in the particularities but in the overarching reason for the laws—namely, *a good and just society*. The laws are dedicated to care of neighbor, fair treatment, compensation for offenses, and general well-being. Sin is generally defined by what harms others. This overarching intent of the laws is confirmed by two words that the Deuteronomic law uses to describe the governing criteria for Israel's society: righteousness (*tsedeq*) and justice (*mishpat*) (Deut. 16:18–19). These two terms are also used in reference to key leaders, from Abraham to King David to the Messiah.[8] In fact, the foundation of God's throne is righteousness and justice (Ps. 89:14).

For some of us, negative church experiences have caused the word "righteousness" to be associated with perfectionism or punitive, rule-based religion. But the Hebrew word connotes a level, clear pathway stretching straight ahead.[9] Biblically, it is associated with light, joy, peace, and healing (e.g., Ps. 97:11; Prov. 4:18; Isa. 32:17; Mal. 4:2). Righteousness is when all is right and well with the world. As Psalm 85:10 puts it, "Righteousness and well-being [*shalom*] kiss each other" (my translation).[10] Similarly, the Hebrew word for justice conveys the idea of a court judgment rendered with equity and untainted by bribes.[11] It is often used in reference to helping someone who is disadvantaged or mistreated by those in power (e.g., Deut. 24:17; 27:19; Ps. 82:3; Isa. 1:17).

Thus, whether and how we apply a particularity from scriptural mandates depends on the underlying intent of the law and its relationship to fostering a good and just world. For example, the reason that Israelite law might require a young woman to marry her rapist was, surprisingly enough, to hold the rapist accountable. Loss of virginity made a woman unmarriageable. In a culture where a woman's identity was rooted in marriage and motherhood, the law was meant to protect her from a desolate future. (See Tamar's response to rape in 2 Sam. 13.) It also protected her father from financial loss. He could lose a dowry and incur costs of supporting his daughter for life—economic circumstances he might not have the resources to sustain. Today, we still strive to hold rapists accountable and protect women's well-being. But we do so in alternative ways that actually *enhance* that intent. We have imagined possibilities for better supporting women in that situation.

The Old Testament laws are not irrelevant, as progressives tend to argue. Neither are the laws impervious proof texts for ethical behavior, as traditionalists sometimes claim. On the one hand, if we ignore certain scriptural texts as simply archaic, we miss out on important theological truths. On the other, if we ascribe greater importance to the particularities than to the purpose of the laws, we fall short of God's vision. What both progressives and traditionalists typically overlook is the deliberative process that we must undertake to rightly interpret and apply biblical laws today. That means the Levitical prohibition on male same-sex relations requires prayerful discernment. What is the overarching intent of the Bible's sexual laws? Are there alternative ways to fulfill that intent more fully that take into consideration the predicament of gay and lesbian people?

Summing It Up

Understanding the historical-cultural background and narrative context of Old Testament laws, as well as how inspiration occurred, allows us to appreciate the ethical significance of the text. What is inspired is not the genre or particular ancient Near Eastern legal concerns but rather what the laws signify: a good and just world. Quoting the Old Testament, Jesus made the same point: all the law can be summed up in love of God and love of neighbor (Matt. 22:37–40; see Deut. 6:5 and Lev. 19:18). Jesus didn't dismiss the Old Testament statutes as irrelevant. Rather, he saw past the cultural trappings to affirm the overarching intent and purpose of the laws.

This has important implications for how we use Old Testament mandates in the debate on same-sex relationships. Discernment is required to determine whether and how a biblical directive contributes to the creation of a good and just world. In the next chapter, I discuss how to engage this deliberative process by looking to the biblical authors and Jesus as examples. They teach us how to appropriate ethics from Scripture.

FURTHER READING

Bill T. Arnold and Bryan E. Beyer. *Readings from the Ancient Near East: Primary Sources for Old Testament Study.* Grand Rapids: Baker Academic, 2002.

Samuel A. Jackson. *A Comparison of Ancient Near Eastern Law Collections Prior to the First Millennium BC.* Piscataway, NJ: Gorgias Press, 2008.

Fifty Shekels for Rape? Making Sense of Old Testament Laws

Bernard M. Levinson. *Legal Revision and Religious Renewal in Ancient Israel.* Cambridge: Cambridge University Press, 2008.

Martha T. Roth. *Law Collections from Mesopotamia and Asia Minor.* Edited by Piotr Michalowski. Atlanta: Scholars Press, 1995.

Raymond Westbrook, ed. *A History of Ancient Near Eastern Law.* 2 vols. Leiden: Brill, 2003.

5

What Is Ethical?
Interpreting the Bible like Jesus

One of the challenges of using the Bible for ethics is determining when a value is culturally bound and when it's enduring. Progressives assert that the biblical prohibitions against same-sex relationships reflect the cultural situation of the biblical authors. Traditionalists are uneasy with such arguments out of concern for the authority of Scripture. At the same time, many traditionalists do recognize that the Bible has a cultural context. Most conservative churches do not require women to wear head coverings.[1] Sermons against sex with a menstruating woman are unheard of despite the prohibition appearing in the same Levitical list as same-sex relations. And egalitarian traditionalists readily support women in leadership in the face of 1 Timothy 2:12. While traditionalists *do* understand some directives as culturally relative, they don't accept this argument when it comes to same-sex relationships. Why not? Traditionalists believe a creation ordinance is an absolute and unchangeable ethic.[2] How God ordered the universe transcends culture. The question now is whether this conclusion is always warranted. In light of this, let's explore how we draw ethics from Scripture.

How Do We Get Ethics from the Bible?

"For the Bible tells me so." That is a familiar refrain for those of us who grew up in the church. The song lyric gives reassuring confidence that "Jesus loves me, this I know." Scripture is full of wonderful affirmations about God's kindness toward us. Those who consider the Bible authoritative find great joy and meaning in it precisely because its divine inspiration makes those assertions trustworthy. The phrase "for the Bible tells me so" also conveys the idea that the Bible tells us what to *do*. But in what sense does the Bible give us specific directions for how to act?

Ever since scriptural texts were written, readers have developed interpretative strategies to determine whether God thinks a particular action or attitude is acceptable. Some of these strategies are easy to spot, such as directly applying a law from the Bible's legal texts. Other approaches are more nuanced. As a starting point, below are four examples illustrating how a person might determine ethics from Scripture:

1. *Commands/rules.* The Bible contains direct commands such as "Do not curse the deaf or put a stumbling block in front of the blind, but fear your God. I am the LORD" (Lev. 19:14). As a result, many Christians have approached the Bible as a rulebook. It's true that many biblical commands are still relevant today. However, reading Scripture solely this way is insufficient. As we saw in the last chapter, the particularities of the biblical laws were influenced by culture and even adapted from other nations. We have to look at the overarching intention of the laws, which was a just and righteous society. In terms of the Levitical law against male same-sex relations, the question is whether traditionalists or progressives have examined the command in terms of its applicability for a just society today.

2. *Exemplar.* Throughout Jewish and Christian history, the lives of biblical figures have been used as examples to follow: "Imitate

Esther, who was brave and saved her people," or "Be like David, who was repentant," or "Notice Mary's humility, and surrender to God's will." A traditionalist might encourage gay people to look at Paul as an example of a celibate man who lived a self-sacrificial life. A progressive might highlight Ruth's covenant loyalty to Naomi and the God of Israel.

3. *Symbolic worlds.* Traditionalist Richard Hays points out that the key passage in the debate on same-sex relationships, Romans 1, doesn't list any commands.[3] If the Bible is to be read strictly as a rulebook, then this passage would not apply to the discussion. What this passage does is provide a perceptual world to frame how we might live our lives. For example, worshiping something other than God (i.e., idolatry) is clearly pictured as human depravity. Another example of a symbolic world is Genesis 1–3, which traditionalists interpret as portraying an ethic of male-female complementarity and procreative union. Progressives, on the other hand, more frequently turn to Galatians 3:28, where they find a symbolic world that transcends categories of male and female.

4. *Virtues.* The Bible names specific virtues. For example, "But the fruit of the Spirit is love, joy, peace, forbearance, kindness, goodness, faithfulness, gentleness, and self-control. Against such things there is no law" (Gal. 5:22–23). Appropriating ethics from Scripture based on virtues means paying attention not only to outward actions but also to the heart. Virtues are about *who* a person is, whereas rules address *what* a person does. Good character is the fountain from which ethical behavior flows. Paul teaches that "there is no law" against the fruit of the Spirit (v. 23). Both traditionalists and progressives can agree on biblical virtues.

Are Same-Sex Relationships Virtuous?

From the above examples, ethics based on virtues is especially help-ful for the conversation, for two reasons. First, virtue is not cul-turally relative in a way that a law might be. The fruit of the Spirit transcends all time and culture. Second, virtue includes the other approaches (i.e., command, exemplar, and symbolic worlds). Con-sider the virtue of love: the *command* "Love your neighbor" is still relevant because the virtue of love is enduring; Jesus is an *exemplar* of love we can imitate, whether washing feet or dying for another; and 1 John paints a *symbolic world* where human love gives us a window to see and experience God (4:12).

In the debate on same-sex relationships, progressives make a compelling argument from virtue ethics.[4] If sin is defined as something that violates the fruit of the Spirit, how are loving, monogamous same-sex relationships sinful? These partnerships are fully capable of exhib-iting the fruit of the Spirit. If Jesus says that all the law can be summed up in love, then don't these relationships meet that requirement? Paul says, "The only thing that counts is faith expressing itself through love" (Gal. 5:6). The whole purpose of the law *is* to teach us to love one an-other (Rom. 13:8–10). Jesus indicates that if we act out of virtue, the outcome is always the will of God. He said, "But give from your heart to those in need, and then everything will be clean for you" (Luke 11:41 NET). Jesus made this statement to religious leaders who assumed that outward performance of rules and rituals made them pure before God. But Jesus explained that having an inward disposition of care for others is what matters. When the virtue of selfless love fills a person's heart, all actions that flow from that are pure and pleasing to God.

The virtue ethics argument is compelling, especially in light of the discussion on law in the previous chapter. But many traditional-ists are uneasy with this approach. Part of this discomfort stems from hesitancy to put virtue ethics and biblical commands in opposition.[5] Progressives might respond to this concern by saying that the Bible does not speak to covenanted same-sex relationships and thus we can feel confident in discerning God's will on the basis of virtues. In this they are correct: the Bible doesn't address covenanted same-sex relationships as we know them today. But the argument is one from silence. Given that some negative assessment of same-sex relations exists in the Bible, traditionalists prefer to err on the side of caution. Traditionalists also base their sexual ethics on God's design for creation. Genesis states that God made male and female. Such a design is deemed an immutable mandate for all sexual relationships.[6]

I would like to present an argument that speaks to the continued concerns that traditionalists have—one that does *not* put law and virtue at odds. The biblical authors themselves show us how to do this. The way they interpreted divine revelation to apply ethics provides a model for us as we contemplate the ethical question of same-sex relationships—namely, *biblical mandates, including creation ordinances, require a deliberative process.*

How Did the Biblical Authors Apply Ethics from Scripture?

One thing I was never taught in Sunday school is that the biblical authors interpreted earlier divine revelation in fresh ways. Like most people who grow up in conservative evangelical circles, I viewed the Bible as static. That is, I assumed each book of the Bible had been written by one particular author (Moses, Ezekiel, etc.) who submitted his work in final form to what we now call the Bible. In my mind, the words were set in stone, carefully penned during moments of direct revelation, with no editing necessary. But as I went on to study the Bible, I learned something fascinating: the Bible is a document characterized by various layers and edits that occurred as it was passed down over hundreds of years.

In antiquity, writing was done in short spurts on clay, papyrus, or animal skin. Bound books did not yet exist. What I discovered was that the Bible is a collection of many different texts pieced together like a quilt. Various scribes copied, edited, and compiled these texts over

hundreds of years. For anyone who takes the time to study this phenomenon, hundreds of editorial marks can be spotted. For example, in
the Masoretic (Hebrew) Text of Isaiah 2:9–11, a scribe added sentences
(intensifying God's wrath) that are not found in the Great Isaiah Scroll
from Qumran (our oldest manuscript of Isaiah).[7] These additions are
preserved in our modern Bibles. In fact, we even have two different
books of Jeremiah, providing us a major example of scribal work in
progress.[8] Jeremiah's oracles were compiled and edited distinctly by
different scribes. This probably occurred because of the exile, when
Jews were dispersed to various locations. The Greek translation of
Jeremiah is based on a Hebrew manuscript that is older and shorter
than the Masoretic Text,[9] which we have in our modern Bibles today.

Biblical scribes felt comfortable not only editing and adding
commentary to scriptural texts passed down to them, but also offer-
ing fresh interpretations. They respected and retained older revelation while contemplating how it related to their contemporary situations. Even divinely inspired laws could be changed.[10] For example,
the writer of Deuteronomy altered the slavery laws in Exodus. He
read the old law in a fresh way that allowed the intention of the
mandates to be fulfilled in his contemporary context. As you read
these passages below, notice the distinctions. The italicized phrases
highlight the differences between the two texts.

Exodus 21:2–11:

If you buy *a [male] Hebrew [slave]*, he is to serve you for
six years.[11] But in the seventh year, *he shall go free*, without paying anything. If he comes alone, he is to go free
alone; but if he has a wife when he comes, she is to go
with him. If his master gives him a wife and she bears
him sons or daughters, the woman and her children shall
belong to her master, and only the man shall go free. But
if the [slave] declares, "I love my master and my wife and
children and do not want to go free," then his master must
take him before the judges. He shall take him to the door

or the doorpost and pierce his ear with an awl. Then he
will be his [slave] for life.

*If a man sells his daughter as a [slave], she is not to go free
as male [slaves] do.* If she does not please the master who
has selected her for himself, he must let her be redeemed.
He has no right to sell her to foreigners, because he has broken faith with her. If he selects her for his son, he must grant
her the rights of a daughter. If he marries another woman,
he must not deprive the first one of her food, clothing, and
marital rights. If he does not provide her with these three
things, she is to go free, without any payment of money.

Deuteronomy 15:12–18:
If any of your people—*Hebrew men or women*—sell themselves to you and serve you six years, in the seventh year
you must let them go free.[12] *And when you release them, do
not send them away empty-handed. Supply them liberally
from your flock, your threshing floor, and your winepress.
Give to them as the Lord your God has blessed you. Remember that you were slaves in Egypt* and the LORD your God
redeemed you. That is why I give you this command today.
But if your [slave] says to you, "I do not want to leave you,"
because he loves you and your family and is well off with
you, then take an awl and push it through his earlobe into
the door, and he will become your [slave] for life.

*Do the same for your female [slave]. Do not consider it
a hardship to set your [slave] free, because their service to
you these six years has been worth twice as much as that
of a hired hand.* And the LORD your God will bless you
in everything you do.

As we read these passages closely, we discover that the author
of Deuteronomy provided a fresh interpretation of the law on slavery.[13] In Exodus only male slaves are permitted to go free after six

years. The updated law in Deuteronomy applies freedom equally to female slaves. This new provision also improves the circumstances for slaves. A male slave is not forced to leave behind a wife, since both male and female slaves are freed after six years. A female slave is not subject to the whims of the owner. She gets to decide if she wants to stay or not. If she does stay, she is to be treated with the same regard as a male slave. The reinterpretation also requires the owner to give an abundance of provisions to help slaves reestablish themselves.[14] Moreover, the author of Deuteronomy is concerned about attitude, desiring the owner to empathize with his slaves ("*Remember that you were slaves*"), appreciate what the slaves provided over six years of service, and release them without any resentment.[15]

How is it that the biblical author felt comfortable adapting divine revelation? According to Exodus, the original slavery law was given directly by God on Mount Sinai: "The LORD said to Moses . . . These are the laws you are to set before them" (see Exod. 19:18–21:11 for context). Notably, the original law gives a prohibition: the female slave "shall not go out as the male slaves do" (Exod. 21:7). This prohibition is overturned in Deuteronomy. The biblical authors understood the nature and function of revelation in a way that is different from what many of us have been taught in our churches. They did not view it as inflexible and impervious.[16] Rather, they understood that laws need to be interpreted with discernment, not blindly applied without regard for context. The intent of the original statute was to provide certain protections for slaves; the adapted law *enhances* that objective by expressing *greater* care for the people involved.

We see a similar interpretive principle at work in the New Testament when it comes to laws on divorce. At first it seems that Jesus tightens divorce laws such that no further discussion should be had (Mark 10:2–12). In fact, he says that Moses allowed an accommodation of divorce only because of hardness of heart (v. 5).[17] But the New Testament authors do not interpret Jesus's strong statement as a reason to blindly apply it. Here we see how the original teaching

SCRIPTURE, ETHICS, AND SAME-SEX RELATIONSHIPS

in Mark (the earliest written Gospel) is interpreted by the author of Matthew's Gospel and by Paul.[18]

Author of Mark (10:11–12):
He answered, "Anyone who divorces his wife and marries another woman commits adultery against her. And if she divorces her husband and marries another man, she commits adultery."

Author of Matthew (19:9):
I tell you that anyone who divorces his wife, *except for sexual immorality [porneia]*, and marries another woman commits adultery.

Paul (1 Cor. 7:12–15):
To the rest I say this (I, not the Lord) . . . *if the [unbelieving spouse] leaves, let it be so. The brother or the sister is not bound in such circumstances.*

The original teaching did not specify any exceptions for divorce. However, Matthew and Paul both add exceptions. Matthew allows divorce in cases of unchastity, and Paul allows divorce if a spouse is abandoned. Like the author of Deuteronomy, they did not blindly apply law without discernment. If we are to consider these biblical authors inspired, then these exceptions do not reflect the hardness of heart that Jesus was referring to in relation to Moses. What might have been the difference? Moses's law allowed a man to divorce if he found "something indecent" (*'erwat dabar*) about his wife (Deut. 24:1–4). The ambiguity in this allowance resulted in men divorcing their wives for even trivial reasons.[19] Jesus addresses that abuse. When Matthew and Paul interpret Jesus's mandate, they do not trivialize it. They affirm that couples should not divorce. So their interpretive method is not a rejection of law. Rather, they employ a deliberative method to discern *how* a law is to be applied.

They realize that to arrive at the will of God, nuanced application is necessary. To apply law indiscriminately can lead to cruel outcomes that God never intended.

One more thing to notice about Jesus's teaching on divorce: it is grounded in a creation ordinance (Mark 10:6–8). One might think that would settle the matter, with no further discussion required. But we see that the biblical authors did not consider that a reason to forgo a discernment process. Paul encountered a situation that Jesus had not addressed: Christian converts married to unbeliev- ers. To properly apply scriptural mandates, he had to engage in a deliberative process to determine how best to do so in his particular context. Both Matthew and Paul upheld the teaching on divorce while attending to the needs of victims in a marital tragedy (betrayal or abandonment).

Key Interpretive Principle: Discernment of Human Need

We learn from the biblical authors that to apply Scripture properly to our lives, we need to bring its teaching into conversation with context and employ careful discernment. But how can we be sure we are applying Scripture correctly and not just interpreting the Bible according to our own whims? The above examples give guidance. In the case of slavery conditions and divorce, the interpretive key is attention to human need. Preexisting divine revelation was applied with a pastoral eye for the suffering of those involved.

Let's look at a few more examples to explore this point. We have seen that the biblical authors interpret scriptural texts with consideration for circumstances. Jesus also states that violation of law in and of itself does not always constitute sin. Context, in which we pay attention to human need, affects how sin is defined. In one instance, Jesus readily admits that David violated the law when he and his companions ate sacred bread that only priests were permit- ted to eat (Matt. 12:3–4). According to Levitical law, the tabernacle bread was the most holy portion the priest could eat from the offerings to God (Lev. 24:5–9). Only the descendants of Aaron could lawfully consume it. So, why does Jesus excuse what David did? *Because David was hungry.*

We see a similar example in how Jesus addresses the Sabbath law. Jesus did not actually break the Sabbath law as he was accused of doing (more on this below). But he responds to his accusers on the terms of their objections. In other words, he doesn't reply, "Well, technically I didn't violate it. Let me parse it out for you." Instead, he takes seriously their concern about properly applying law. He teaches them that attention to need is necessary to rightly employ scriptural mandates. He gives specific examples, such as helping an animal or a person who is suffering (Matt. 12:9–13), or freeing a man who hasn't walked in thirty-eight years to finally pick up and carry his mat (John 5:5–9).

Jesus essentially says, yes, hypothetically even *if* he had violated the Sabbath law, God's law cannot be applied accurately without a deliberative process. And yes, David violated the law, but given his circumstances, the overall intent of God's law was best upheld by attending to human need. In other words, Jesus teaches us that when we derive ethics from Scripture, it is always "lawful to do good" (Matt. 12:12). The laws hadn't changed—the bread was still only for the priests to eat, and Sabbath was still on the books—but *how* to apply these mandates was discerned by taking into account people's suffering or need (e.g., slavery conditions, abuse in marriage, hunger, illness).

What about a Creation Ordinance?

The biblical authors used discernment even for laws based on a creation ordinance, namely, the permanency of marriage. So also Sabbath law is grounded in creation. The Israelites were given the Sabbath law because "in six days the LORD made the heavens and the earth, and on the seventh day he rested and was refreshed" (Exod. 31:17; see 20:10–11; 31:16–17; also Gen. 2:1–3 and Isa. 58).[20] Just as with same-sex relations, violating this law demanded the death penalty (Exod. 31:12–15). Contrary to popular belief, Jesus did not do away with the Sabbath. In fact, it was his custom to observe it (Luke 4:16). After Jesus's death, his most intimate followers honored the Sabbath even when it meant waiting to care for his body (Mark 16:1). This is not what we would expect from his disciples if Jesus had taught that the Sabbath is no longer relevant.

Even though Jesus honored the Sabbath, he was accused of violating it. In response to his accusers, he took their objections at face value and taught *the fundamental reason* for God's law, namely, God's law is made for humankind, not humankind for God's law (Mark 2:27). In other words, God's ordinances are always *on behalf of* people and not for the arbitrary appeasement of God's sensibilities. For that reason, even a creation ordinance requires discernment to be properly interpreted and applied. Lest we think such interpretative work was only for the inspired biblical authors, Jesus indicates otherwise. His instructions for interpreting the Bible were given to ordinary religious leaders of his day (i.e., the faith community). He confronted them for failing to adequately engage the deliberative process. In other words, the interpretive practices we see Jesus and the biblical authors employ are examples given for us to follow. Jesus wanted his accusers to learn how to be better readers and appliers of Scripture.

Paul provides another example of how to interpret a creation ordinance in congruence with Jesus's teaching. Like Jesus, Paul regularly observed the Sabbath (Acts 17:1–2; 18:4), but he recognized that humankind was not made to blindly and slavishly employ Sabbath laws. Human need matters when applying biblical law. Thus, Paul countered legalistic application of it. Specifically, he countered teachers promoting harsh treatment of the body and rule-based religion (Col. 2:8–23). Observing the harsh treatment, he counsels, "do not let anyone judge you with respect to food or drink, or in the matter of a feast, new moon, or Sabbath days—these are only the shadow of the things to come" (vv. 16–17 NET). Paul reminds his audience that the Sabbath, among other observances, is meant to help us see God. It foreshadows or points to the glorious new heaven and new earth. It witnesses to and symbolizes spiritual truth. The writer of Hebrews reiterates this: "The law possesses a shadow of the good things to come" (10:1 NET).

Paul's point about symbolism is important to the debate on same-sex relationships. Traditionalists frequently argue that male and female must be upheld for marriage because this distinction symbolizes spiritual realities. It points to the eschatological wedding between Christ and the church or the Trinitarian relationship. Yet Paul counsels us not to confuse the symbol with the real thing. To slavishly uphold the symbol without regard for circumstances is wrong. Paul, following Jesus, teaches that attention to need is more important than practicing a symbol that witnesses to heaven. Why? Because mercy toward human suffering *is* the point. The eschatological wedding *is* the ultimate celebration of no more "mourning and crying and pain" (Rev. 21:3–4).

Summing It Up

Traditionalists assert that same-sex relationships are always prohibited because the proscription is based on a creation ordinance. In this chapter we looked at this assumption and found that, according to the biblical authors, a creation ordinance in and of itself does not mean we can neglect the deliberative process in applying biblical mandates today. In fact, blindly applying law without discernment violates the very purpose of God's law, which Jesus states is given *on behalf of* humankind. The biblical authors show us by example how to go about this discernment process. Mandates are applied with attention to human need and suffering. This means that when we are confronted with an ethical question, we must prayerfully consider the needs of those involved. In the case of same-sex relationships, we might consider how the needs of gay and lesbian people nuance application of the biblical prohibition, particularly concerning the expectation of lifelong celibacy.[21]

FURTHER READING

John Barton. *Ethics in Ancient Israel.* Oxford: Oxford University Press, 2014.

Charles Cosgrove. *Appealing to Scripture in the Moral Debate: Five Hermeneutical Rules.* Grand Rapids: Eerdmans, 2002.

Lúcás Chan. *Biblical Ethics in the 21st Century: Developments, Emerging Consensus, and Future Directions.* Mahwah, NJ: Paulist, 2013.

Bernard M. Levinson. *Legal Revision and Religious Renewal in Ancient Israel.* Cambridge: Cambridge University Press, 2008.

Mark Noll. *The Civil War as a Theological Crisis.* Chapel Hill: University of North Carolina Press, 2006. While I believe this author is a traditionalist, this book is one of the most compelling for the progressive argument. It shows how Scripture has been used in a legalistic fashion. Although slavery was technically never outlawed entirely in the Bible, arguments in favor of it missed the spirit and essence of the whole law: love your neighbor. The book will be thought-provoking for anyone interested in sound interpretation of the Bible.

Luke Timothy Johnson. *Scripture and Discernment: Decision-Making in the Church.* Nashville: Abingdon, 1996.

6

The Question of Celibacy
for Gay and Lesbian People

Does the difficulty of lifelong celibacy provide biblical grounds for considering same-sex relationships morally acceptable? Traditionalists typically answer this question negatively on the basis of the biblical prohibitions. They might empathize with the suffering of lifelong celibacy, but violating a rule just feels wrong—even when Jesus and the biblical authors apply law with discernment and nuance. Better to play it safe. I can certainly relate to that desire to be cautious. Yet to err on the side of indiscriminate application of law is to fall prey to the same temptation as the religious leaders of Jesus's day. They didn't want to get it wrong, but their zeal ensured that they did. Jesus and the biblical authors show us a different way that is more faithful to God and to Scripture. They invite us to engage the crucial deliberative process for applying biblical mandates.

It might be challenging for some traditionalists to fathom a situation where same-sex relationships are morally acceptable, but conservatives *do* make exceptions to the rule for other major controversial issues. For example, conservatives adamantly oppose abortion, calling it murder. But Focus on the Family recognizes that in some cases abortion may be ethical for humanitarian reasons: "We would not consider it immoral for a woman to accept treatment that is necessary to save her life, but which may end the life of her preborn child."[1] Significantly, this statement affirms the possibility that what is normally considered sin is no longer immoral in a particular context. An exception to the rule is made on humanitarian grounds. This dovetails with exceptions we find in Scripture, as discussed in the previous chapter.

In addition to humanitarian grounds, the morality of same-sex relationships can be assessed through casuistry (the development of case law). This refers to the process of extrapolating ethics from existing principles in Scripture to resolve an ethical dilemma that is not directly addressed in the Bible. Specifically, Paul never addresses the situation of a gay person who is unable to achieve celibacy. Paul instructs the church: "Now to the unmarried and the widows I say . . . if they cannot control themselves, they should marry, for it is better to marry than to burn with passion" (1 Cor. 7:9). How might this teaching be applied to gay and lesbian people who cannot function in a heterosexual marriage?

The Presbyterian Church in America (PCA) provides a helpful example of how to apply a deliberative process. The PCA, a conservative evangelical denomination, conducted an in-depth deliberative process to determine what constitutes biblical grounds for divorce. In doing so, they observed: "Scripture does not address the circumstance of an abusive husband. As is the case in any other area of Biblical ethics, one cannot extract from Scripture a comprehensive statement of all possible applications of a divine law. Rather, it is left to the church to apply Biblical norms, with the direction provided by the casuistry Scripture does supply, to the untold number of situations which must be faced."[2]

The PCA studied opinions of Reformed theologians and analyzed relevant biblical texts. They took note of sixteenth-century Puritan preacher William Perkins's interpretation of Paul's exception to divorce in the case of abandonment by an unbelieving spouse (1 Cor. 7:15). Perkins applied this text to domestic violence: "For to depart from one [abandonment], and drive away by threats, are equipollent [equivalent]."[3] The PCA committee agreed: "A husband's

SCRIPTURE, ETHICS, AND SAME-SEX RELATIONSHIPS

violence . . . , if unremedied, seems to us, by any application of Biblical norms, to be as much a ruination of the marriage in fact as adultery or actual departure. This is so precisely because his violence separates them, either by her forced withdrawal from the home or by the profound cleavage between them which the violence produces, as surely as would his own departure, and is thus an expression of his unwillingness 'to consent' to live with her in marriage (1 Cor. 7:12–13; Eph. 5:28–29)."[4] The PCA allows victims of unremedied domestic violence to lawfully divorce and remarry.

The question of same-sex relationships warrants the same attentive deliberative process, especially as it relates to the feasibility of lifelong celibacy. As discussed in Chapter 1, most Christians throughout history have assumed that people who engage in same-sex relations do so as a result of spiritual depravity or mental illness. Thus, a person need only to repent or find healing and resume a normal heterosexual life, allowing marriage to the opposite sex. But these assumptions have proven false. In the rest of this chapter, I provide evidence to support the assertion that same-sex relationships can be considered morally acceptable based on case law (Paul's instructions on celibacy and marriage), as well as on the basis of the humanitarian exception to the rule.

The Truth about Sexual Orientation Change

When I contemplate lifelong celibacy, I feel both joy and sorrow. Joy when I think of Mother Teresa or theologian John Stott, both self-sacrificial people whose celibacy enhanced their life's work. Wesley Hill also comes to mind, a celibate gay professor of New Testament who has blessed the church with a rich theology of friendship and community. But my heart is sorrowful when I think of Ryan Robertson, a young man who grew up in a loving evangelical family and didn't have the strength to bear the burden imposed on him by his conservative community.[5] For years he received counseling and earnestly prayed for healing. The inability to change his sexual orientation and face life without a family of his own became too much. Desperate and depressed, he self-medicated the pain with drugs and died of an overdose at the age of twenty.

Lifelong celibacy is beautiful and meaningful for those who have the grace and call for it. But it can lead to physical and emotional death for those who do not. In the discussion on same-sex relationships, traditionalists have not adequately wrestled with the question of permanent sexual abstinence. Is lifelong celibacy achievable for *anyone* who attempts it (including an entire demographic, comprising millions of people)? Traditionalists frequently sidestep these questions, as two recent books by traditionalists have done, by focusing attention on sexual orientation change and mixed orientation marriages before giving cursory attention to lifelong celibacy.[6]

Research has confirmed that change in sexual orientation (that might enable a healthy heterosexual marriage) is uncommon.[7] This is the conclusion of not only progressive scholars but also conservatives who hold a traditionalist view. Almost twenty years ago, evangelicals Dr. Stanton Jones (Wheaton College) and Dr. Mark Yarhouse (Regent University) admitted, "However the orientation toward homosexual preference develops, there is substantial agreement that it is not a preference that can be easily changed by the simple act of the will."[8]

Seven years after they penned the above statement, Jones and Yarhouse conducted a longitudinal study with ex-gays who attended Exodus support groups.[9] While they knew that sexual orientation does not readily change, they wanted to test progressive claims that sexual orientation can *never* change or that attempts at change always cause harm. While the study results did not indicate that participants experienced harm, shifts in sexual orientation were quite low. Only 23 percent reported a shift after six years of trying, and most of the change was toward bisexuality (or "complicated heterosexuality," as the authors put it). This percentage is likely optimistic, since several study participants dropped out before it was completed. In other words, even an optimistic view suggests that nearly 80 percent of gay people will *not* experience a change in sexual orientation despite years of actively attempting to do so.

In 2014 Mormon psychologist Dr. John Dehlin and his colleagues published a large study surveying 1,612 current or former members of the Mormon Church (where motivation to change is high).[10] Only 1 out of 1,019 respondents who had attempted to change reported a shift to heterosexuality (0.1 percent). Participants also reported negative effects from the attempts.

Recently, Dr. Warren Throckmorton, an evangelical psychologist who previously believed sexual orientation was amenable to change, summed up scholarly consensus:

> I think most therapists now understand that sexual orientation is durable and rarely, if ever, changes dramatically as the result of change therapy. . . .
>
> As for the goal of ending change therapy for youth, I am a supporter. Despite years of research and effort, no safe, effective and ethical approach to sexual orientation change has emerged. The very few people who still claim effectiveness are [part of] small operations with no research of their own methods. The anecdotes of harm are convincing and the candid admissions of people like Alan Chambers that the change they claimed didn't happen is enough to cause significant skepticism. My own professional experience researching change efforts in clients and research participants informs me that any claimed change is unlikely to be lasting or complete. The biological research, while not conclusive, supports a very early establishment of sexual desires (especially for males).[11]

This is not to discount those who profess a change in orientation. However, those testimonies represent a small minority.[12] As traditionalists increasingly come to terms with the truth that sexual orientation change is unlikely for the overwhelming majority, those who oppose same-sex relationships need to engage in a robust conversation on the feasibility of lifelong celibacy.

Single People Today

One common argument that traditionalists make is that gay people are no different than straight people who can't find a mate and must remain chaste. This assertion has significant problems. First, saying no to temptation is not as difficult when no one is available to tempt one's desires; it's a different story to resist the love of one's life. When straight people fall in love, they marry. When gay people fall in love, they must find the herculean strength to say no, not only in the moment of desire, but to every dream of marriage and family. Second, a profound difference exists between someone who happens to be single but can actively pursue dating and marriage and someone who is forbidden to do either. How many heterosexual singles are willing to cease dating, give up the hope of marriage, and make a lifetime vow of celibacy? Not many. Yet that is essentially what traditionalists are requiring gay people to do.

Third, and perhaps most significantly, straight, unmarried people often *don't* succeed at celibacy. While some straight people might have the ability to live in permanent sexual abstinence, not everyone can. In fact, "single" is a misnomer, since many unmarried heterosexuals, including Christians, are dating, cohabitating, or otherwise involved in romantic or sexual relationships. In other words, arguing that gay people must be celibate because heterosexuals also need to be chaste ignores the reality that many straight people are equally unable to achieve lifelong celibacy. This cannot be blamed only on moral weakness. Rather, God designed human beings for intimate relations. Lifelong celibacy is an atypical state that goes against our biology.

Learning to control our sex drive is part of maturity, but puberty creates real changes in the body that impel us. Physical and emotional attractions to another person, which are rarely conjured by choice, change our chemistry such that resisting mutual affection often requires significant external support. That's why even devout teenagers who sign virginity pledges are, statistically, only able to hold out eighteen months longer.[13] By the age of twenty-one, they are just as likely to have had sex as non-pledgers.[14] Focus on the Family's publication for youth counsels readers to marry young in full recognition that prolonged attempts at chastity are unrealistic.[15] Studies of evangelicals between ages eighteen to twenty-nine show rates of nonmarital sex at 44–80 percent.[16] Similarly, an evaluation of Catholic priests indicates achieving lifelong celibacy is difficult even for those who actively choose it. Psychotherapist Richard Sipe, a Benedictine monk for eighteen years, estimates that up to 50 percent of Catholic priests are involved in sexual activity at some point in their career.[17]

Some voices argue that we do not need sex for human flourishing, and we only think we do because we live in a hypersexualized culture. I understand why this argument is made. We have an unprecedented number of unmarried people in our society. The church wants to encourage singles who feel alienated by the idolization of marriage. And certainly the value of lifelong celibacy (for those who have the grace and call) has not received due esteem. But the reality is that human beings are biologically made for sexual relationships, not lifelong celibacy. Pretending that this is not true will only enhance the disorder evident since the sexual revolution. People *will* have sex either within marriage or outside it. Once we appreciate (not deny or fear) the way we are wired as sexual creatures, we can have reasonable conversations about what it means to live in this world as it is. For a church that cares about sexual holiness, that means inspiring loyal, covenanted love.

Christian Tradition on Celibacy

Lifelong celibacy is possible for *some* people. Many religious traditions around the world honor the practice, especially among their leaders. But the claim that *anyone* can achieve a lifetime of celibacy is not representative of Christian tradition. This recent assertion seems to have developed as a way to counter gay marriage, as well as to make sense of the unusually high number of unmarried people in our modern Western culture. But throughout church history, the answer to the question of universal attainability has been "No." Despite high regard for the celibate life, Christians have readily understood that some are too "weak" and require the accommodation of marriage to live a holy life. The following is a brief overview of Christian tradition on celibacy.

When Jesus and Paul came on the scene, celibacy was an anomaly in Jewish and Greco-Roman cultures. In fact, Roman law penalized those who did not wed and propagate.[18] In early Jewish tradition, marriage and procreation were considered biblical mandates (per Gen. 1:28). Sexual abstinence was permitted or required only temporarily for purity purposes.[19] We see an example of this in the book of Exodus when the Israelites refrain from sex for three days in preparation for God's appearance on Mount Sinai (19:14–15; see also 1 Sam. 21:4).[20] Ancient Jewish commentaries refer to sexual abstinence on the Sabbath or for a period of prayer (*Jubilees* 50:8 and *Testament of Naphtali* 8:8, respectively).

In the New Testament, a similar purity theme appears in Paul's instructions for couples to refrain temporarily from sex for prayer (1 Cor. 7:5), as well as in Revelation's eschatological scene of 144,000 elect male virgins who have "not defiled themselves with women" (14:1–5). But early Christianity did more than affirm temporary abstinence for purity reasons; it saw celibacy as symbolic of the eternal age to come. Traditional Jewish theology envisioned fertility in the eschaton (e.g., Isa. 11:8; Wisdom 3:13; 2 Baruch 73:7), but Jesus said marriage and procreation do not exist in the age to come (Luke

20:34–36). The idea of sexual abstinence in the coming age possibly developed from framing the end of time as the ultimate Sabbath, a holy realm of purity and consecration (e.g., *Jubilees* 50:8 and Heb. 4:8–11), or viewing the new heaven and new earth as a holy space, like the earthly temple, where the presence of God perpetually dwells (Rev. 21:1–3).[21]

Paul also acknowledges that the body is a temple for the Holy Spirit (1 Cor. 6:12–20), and while he gives that as a reason to refrain from sexual immorality, he does not consider celibacy a requirement for Christians to experience God's presence through the Holy Spirit. In fact, he counters Christians who apparently preached mandatory lifelong celibacy in anticipation of the eschaton. These teachers asserted that "it is good for a man not to have sexual relations with a woman" (1 Cor. 7:1). Against this severe asceticism, Paul says that marital sex is important for living a holy life (1 Cor. 7:2–5).

Paul understood the power of the sex drive. While he esteemed celibacy and wished more Christians would embrace that way of life, he readily acknowledged that not everyone has the ability to remain in a permanent state of sexual abstinence. Not only does he tell married couples to employ sex in marriage to reduce temptation (1 Cor. 7:5), but he also urges single people to marry if they cannot achieve celibacy: "But if they cannot control themselves, they should marry, for it is better to marry than to burn with passion. . . . If anyone is worried that he might not be acting honorably toward the virgin he is engaged to, and if his passions are too strong and he feels he ought to marry, he should do as he wants" (vv. 9, 36). For Paul, marriage is vital in helping a person to achieve a holy life. Jesus similarly acknowledges that not everyone can attain lifelong celibacy, but only those to whom it has been given (Matt. 19:10–12). He states that despite the realities of the eschaton, in this present age people marry and are given in marriage (Luke 20:34).

Paul counseled temporary sexual abstinence for purity reasons (prayer), but his motivation for lifelong celibacy was freedom to serve God (1 Cor. 7:32–35; see also Luke 18:29–30). His encouragement to remain unmarried was also influenced by his belief that the eschaton was imminent (1 Cor. 7:29). There was no purpose in getting married and starting families when the Lord was returning any moment. The early church took Paul's example of celibacy, and that of Jesus's, to heart. In doing so, they blended purity reasons for abstinence with those pertaining to service. Ironically, what Paul attempted to correct in his letter to the Corinthians was used to argue for essentially the same thing that the heretics did. Church leaders latched onto Paul's statement of abstaining from sex for prayer, combined it with a separate scripture about praying without ceasing (1 Thess. 5:17), and developed a theology out of it. By the second century, Christians in eastern Syria went so far as to require lifelong celibacy for anyone who received baptism; one had to prove the ability to endure permanent sexual abstinence before undergoing the rite.[22]

Within two hundred years of Jesus and Paul, the church was actively encouraging lifelong celibacy for as many people as possible, including married people. Marriage was considered inferior because it did not reflect the coming age and was thought to be a product of the fall. Sexual differentiation and intercourse became associated with Adam and Eve's disobedience.[23] Psalm 51:5 was employed to argue that parents conceive children through an act of iniquity. In his essay *On Virginity*, Gregory of Nyssa (ca. 335–395 CE) asserted that procreation gives birth to death (mortal children), while those who embrace celibacy give birth to life (spiritual children). On the positive side, the early church considered celibacy to be a way to draw close to God in prayer and to view the world through spiritual eyes. Rather than objectifying other people for one's own desires, celibacy allowed one to love others in a selfless way.

What is striking about this zeal for celibacy, which lasted until the Reformation, is that despite viewing lifelong sexual abstinence as superior to marriage, the same theologians acknowledged that not everyone could attain it. If anyone might have demanded mandatory celibacy, it would have been them (and it essentially came to that in a few extreme cases, such as eastern Syrian Christianity). But the majority considered marriage a legitimate accommodation for weakness. Ambrose writes, "For virginity cannot be commanded, but must be wished for, for things which are above us are matters for prayer rather than under mastery. . . . I do not then discourage marriage, but recapitulate the advantages of holy virginity. This is the gift of few only."[24] Augustine, who esteemed celibacy above marriage, nevertheless acknowledged that marriage serves those who are unable to attain celibacy: "The weakness of both sexes, with its inclination to depravity and ruin, is wisely saved by honorable marriage."[25]

Reformation leader Martin Luther went further than advising marriage as an accommodation and argued for its necessity. From personal experience as a monk, he saw how clergy struggled to keep vows of celibacy. He was also concerned that celibacy had become a type of works righteousness. Luther maintained that no one can be justified by celibacy, but only through faith.[26] If a person chooses celibacy over marriage, he or she does not gain more merit in God's eyes. In fact, Luther argued that the majority of people *should* marry. Celibacy has not played a significant role in the Protestant tradition because of Luther's insistence that we need marriage for a holy life.

Because I believe it is helpful to our discussion on gay people and mandatory celibacy, I provide an extended quotation from Luther below. In doing so, I am not arguing that Luther or other church fathers would have supported same-sex marriage. (I suspect they thought a person with same-sex attractions could just choose heterosexual marriage as an option for sexual release, not truly grasping the nature and durability of sexual orientation.) Rather, I present Luther's comments to further demonstrate the prevalent belief that celibacy is not possible for all people:

> Much as chastity [celibacy] is praised, and no matter how
> noble a gift it is, nevertheless necessity prevails so that

few can attain it, for they cannot control themselves. For although we are Christians and have the spirit of God in faith, still we do not cease to be God's creatures, you a woman, and I a man. And the spirit permits the body its ways and natural functions, so that it eats, drinks, and eliminates like any other human body. . . .

Furthermore, a Christian is spirit and flesh. According to the spirit he has no need of marriage. But because his flesh is the common flesh, corrupted in Adam and Eve and filled with evil desires, therefore because of this very disease, marriage is a necessity for him and it is not in his power to get along without it. For his flesh rages, burns, and fructifies just like that of any other man, unless he helps and controls it with the proper medicine, which is marriage. . . .

Consider how foolish are those teachers and administrators who drive young people to chastity in monasteries and nunneries, claiming that the harder it is for them and the more unwilling they are, the better their chastity is. They should play around with other things and take something besides chastity, for it cannot be voluntary without special grace. . . . For what is it to allow a young person to suffocate in such heat in a monastery or elsewhere his whole life but to burn a child to death in honor of the devil by making it observe a miserable, lost chastity?[27]

Christian tradition from the time of Jesus and Paul has acknowledged that not everyone can be celibate. Even the most zealous church fathers and mothers who viewed celibacy as superior to marriage conceded that marriage is a necessary accommodation. Luther went even further to say that marriage is a necessity and that mandatory celibacy leads to sin and undue suffering. This vast Christian tradition on the infeasibility of celibacy is crucial for the church's ethical discussion on same-sex relationships.

Deliberating on the Morality of Same-Sex Relationships

The assumption in the same-sex marriage debate that lifelong celibacy is possible for everyone is not supported by Christian tradition or social scientific studies. Traditionalists' neglect of a deliberative process that takes this reality into consideration has had tragic consequences. After years of being discouraged and barred from forming covenant partnerships, certain parts of the gay and lesbian community are still grappling with the problem of promiscuity and broken relationships.[28] God created us with a strong familial drive to couple with another person and build a home. Covenant is the means of forming this healthy, lasting relationship. Without it, dysfunction is inevitable.

I invite traditionalists to take into consideration the infeasibility of celibacy (for everyone) in the same way conservatives have considered extenuating circumstances in the deliberative process for divorce and remarriage. Even though conservatives believe divorce is wrong in most cases, they do make allowances for remarriage. When I attended Western Seminary, a conservative Baptist school, one of my professors told the class that after much prayer and pastoral experience with divorced people, he believed Paul's instruction to those with strong passions could be casuistically applied to divorcees. He observed that remarriage is less grievous than repetitive fornication. Notably, Paul never addresses the dilemma of a divorcee who is unable to achieve lifelong celibacy.

Focus on the Family believes people who are unbelievers at the time of divorce are permitted to remarry—an allowance not explicitly stated in Scripture.[29] The PCA not only allows the victim of an adulterous or deserting spouse (or unrepentant abuser) to remarry after divorce, but its pastoral guidelines indicate anyone can remarry if a person's former spouse marries someone else (per case law from Deut. 24:1–4).[30] It also proposes that if a person tries to reconcile with an ex-spouse and the former partner refuses in a manner indicative of being an unbeliever, this constitutes desertion and frees a person to remarry.[31] Furthermore, the PCA concludes that if a person remarries without having biblical grounds, only the first sexual act is adultery; the person does not remain in a perpetual state of sin.[32]

These allowances for remarriage are not attempts to minimize the grievous sin of divorce and its consequences. These conclusions have been carefully drawn from Scripture based on casuistry and demonstrate concern for legitimate human need. The functional result of conservative deliberation on remarriage is that mandatory lifelong celibacy is quite unlikely for someone who divorces. This careful deliberation on divorce and remarriage is in stark contrast to the lack of deliberation on same-sex relationships. This discrepancy stems from traditionalists' bias toward concerns more familiar to the majority of church attenders. Divorce and remarriage are relatable topics, while same-sex attraction is foreign to many leaders who are drafting church position papers. The neglect of gay and lesbian people and their plight reflects traditionalists' grievous disregard of minority church members' needs—not unlike the early church's favoritism of Hebraic widows over Hellenistic widows during food distribution (Acts 6:1–4).

Summing It Up

Traditionalists say the Bible prohibits all same-sex relationships, but they have not engaged the deliberative process. Conservatives deliberate on other controversial issues, allowing that abortion and divorce are morally acceptable in certain contexts. In these situations, conservatives take into account human need, whether the life of a mother or a spouse's well-being in a tragic marriage. In this chapter, I argue that the same deliberation is warranted for same-sex relationships. The infeasibility of celibacy creates a terrible double-bind for the gay person. Unable to achieve celibacy but barred from forming a covenant relationship, a gay person is caught in an impossible situation. Not surprisingly, this can lead to deep depression, suicidal ideation, and self-destructive coping mechanisms. By accepting same-sex covenanted relationships, we take into account the psychological and physical well-being of gay people. If the humanitarian exception to the rule had been offered to Ryan Robertson, the young man described at the beginning of this chapter, he would probably still be alive today.

In addition to humanitarian exceptions to the rule, conservatives regularly extrapolate biblical case law to address ethical questions not answered by Scripture. The PCA's determination that unremedied domestic violence constitutes desertion and grounds for divorce (and remarriage) is one example of this casuistry. Similarly, biblically based casuistry is needed to resolve the ethical dilemma of a gay person unable to achieve celibacy. By extrapolating from Paul's instruction that people with strong passions should marry, a case can be made for the moral acceptability of same-sex covenanted relationships.

FURTHER READING

Raymond F. Collins. *Accompanied by a Believing Wife: Ministry and Celibacy in the Earliest Christian Communities.* Collegeville, MN: Liturgical Press, 2013.

Annemarie S. Kidder. *Women, Celibacy, and the Church.* New York: Crossroad, 2003.

William Loader. *Making Sense of Sex: Attitudes towards Sexuality in Early Jewish and Christian Literature,* 91–104. Grand Rapids: Eerdmans, 2013.

7

Is It Adam's Fault? Why the Origin of Same-Sex Attraction Matters

So far I have made a case for covenanted same-sex relationships from Scripture and Christian tradition. Jesus and the biblical authors teach us how to appropriate ethics from the Bible; namely, mandates cannot be applied indiscriminately, even for creation ordinances. Failure to engage in the deliberative process can lead to an outcome contrary to God's will. Moreover, Christian tradition overwhelmingly recognizes the inability of most people to live a celibate life. One more topic, though, is helpful for considering same-sex partnerships: our concept of the fall and original sin.

If you ask most traditionalists "What causes same-sex attraction?," the bottom-line answer is usually "The fall." Ever since Adam and Eve disobeyed God in the garden, human beings have been prone to sin, and all our desires are distorted. Traditionalists put same-sex attraction in the same category as adulterous thoughts and addiction to pornography. Everyone experiences some form of sexual temptation. For gay people, it happens to be misguided desire for the same sex. Traditionalists typically consider these sexual proclivities symptoms of moral fallenness.

In Christian tradition, the consequences of the fall are twofold: *moral* fallenness, referring to our struggle with sin, and *natural* fallenness as displayed in the fragility of our bodies (e.g., cancer, birth defects, and death). In this chapter, I investigate whether moral fall-enness is the best way to describe same-sex attraction, or whether we might consider it natural fallenness or just human variation. How we categorize same-sex attraction has significant implications for how we respond to gay and lesbian people. But before diving in, let me clarify how categories of moral fallenness and natural fallenness have shown up in theological conversation on same-sex attraction. Below are two examples provided by traditionalists.

Rosaria Butterfield places intersex people (those born with both male and female sex characteristics) in the category of natural fallenness but considers gay people morally fallen. She denies that sexual orientation exists (gay or straight). Instead, she understands all sexual desires and actions as rooted in either holiness or indwelling sin.[1] Butterfield acknowledges scientific evidence of atypical sexual development (intersex conditions). But when it comes to enduring patterns of sexual attraction, she relies on spiritual explanations. Thus, being intersex is not sinful, but the gay person who experiences "unintentional" attraction that "springs up like a hiccup or reflex" exhibits the moral effects of original sin.[2] Butterfield does not discuss the possibility that same-sex attraction is a congenital condition. She addresses outward physical anatomy in relation to natural fallenness, but not the brain's neuroanatomy.[3]

Wesley Hill believes that same-sex relationships are a manifestation of the fall, but denies that all same-sex attraction constitutes moral fallenness.[4] He accepts the American Psychological Association's definition of sexual orientation as encompassing emotional attractions in addition to sexual desire. Everyone's attractions, gay or straight, involve complex affectional aspects that are not necessarily lustful. Hill has a positive view of the "heightened sensitivity to and gifting for non-genital, same-sex friendship" that gay people possess.[5] He argues that Paul did not condemn sexual orientation because the apostle had no concept of it. Contra Butterfield, Hill sees sexual orientation as morally neutral; only same-sex lust and activity are problematic. The question is whether Hill follows his argument to its logical conclusion; namely, if Paul did not grasp the reality of sexual orientation, then possibly the apostle's overall understanding of same-sex attraction is prescientific. In that case, Paul's rebuke of same-sex relations is influenced by his socio-historical context.

So, does Butterfield's proposal of indwelling sin best account for the existence of gay and lesbian people? Does the gay experience contain both fallen and gifted elements, as Hill suggests? Or might same-sex attraction represent variation within human sexual development that is not fallen at all? To explore these questions, we will consider the fall in conversation with science. While scientific research is continually updated, and we need not subject ourselves to every hypothetical whim, science *does* reveal genuine truth about our world and the Creator who made it. In fact, science can help us interpret Scripture and form more accurate theological conclusions.

Human Origins, the Fall, and Biblical Interpretation

One area where science can help us interpret Scripture is human origins as it relates to the Bible's creation stories. If Adam and Eve's sin set in motion all our fallen conditions, moral or natural, it makes sense to ask what science tells us about the first human beings. Below I briefly summarize the theology of the fall and then discuss how we might understand it in light of scientific evidence.

The terms "fall" and "original sin" do not appear in the Bible; the concepts are drawn from interpretations of Scripture, particularly Genesis 3 and Romans 5. The fall refers to a fall from original righteousness. All was right and whole with Adam and Eve when they were created. But after disobeying God by eating the forbidden fruit, they were no longer innocent. This first act of disobedience led to a tragic universal condition affecting all humankind, called "original sin" (originat*ing* with Adam and originat*ed* in us). Genesis 3 does not explicitly say that Adam's error led to originated sin in all his descendants. Nor does Judaism today subscribe to a doctrine of original sin. But many Christians extrapolate the doctrine from Paul's interpretation of Genesis.

Paul writes, "Sin entered the world through one man, and death through sin, and in this way death came to all people, because all sinned" (Rom 5:12). Romans 5 has endured numerous debates and disparate interpretations over the centuries. Augustine believed every human being in history was seminally present in the loins of Adam. In modern terms, that might be expressed as all humanity being genetically present in Adam. Thus, fallenness is transmitted through procreation. Reformed groups suggest the transmission is not so much physical as representative: Adam was the federal or covenant head of humanity; therefore his actions affected all those represented by his headship.

Scientifically, we know Augustine's view is problematic. DNA sequencing shows that human beings did not descend from a single pair. Instead of Adam and Eve, the data indicates Adams and Eves.[6] That is, *Homo sapiens* never existed as a population with less than several thousand people. They also interbred with other *Homo* species, including Neanderthal and Denisovan, now extinct.[7] Thus, we should not imagine that a lone *Homo sapiens* literally passed down every disease or sinful proclivity through procreation. In this sense, same-sex attraction is not physically caused by Adam.

The federal or covenant headship view also runs into challenges. Science does not support the idea of a single *Homo sapiens* as the father of every human being who has ever lived. DNA sequencing can trace humankind back to a common ancestor for males living today, called the "Y-chromosome Adam."[8] However, this man was not the only *Homo sapiens* alive in his time nor the first. In other words, he is only the father of male lineages that happened to survive to the present. Addressing this issue, some theologians suggest Adam was not the first or only human being but rather the first man specially chosen by God to advance divine purposes for humankind, akin to the call of Noah or Abraham. Yet that goes beyond scriptural depictions that clearly portray Adam as the first and lone human being. Such an interpretation accurately recognizes that the biblical authors used literary devices in Genesis, but it doesn't go far enough with the implications of this; namely, that Genesis portrays a theological and not a scientific account of human origins.

In addition to problems with Adam as a physical or representative source of all our struggles, we also have to consider the origin of death, which many have interpreted Paul to say didn't exist until the fall. Yet, both science and Genesis indicate that bodily decay and evil existed prior to Adam.[9] Death, violence, disease, and natural disasters all preceded human beings. One common suggestion to resolve this theological dilemma is that Paul's statement refers to the death of *humankind*. That is, death and turmoil might have been God's design for the animal world, but human beings were originally spared that reality. The problem with this reasoning is that the very design of the universe destines all earthly life to death. The sun is expanding, bringing its heat ever closer to earth. In a few billion years, life on our planet will be destroyed.[10] The terminus date has always been in the cards—long before Adam came along.[11]

If death, including the bodily conditions that lead to death, pre-existed the fall, we might reconsider what physical realities should be labeled "fallen." That is not to say human beings are not fallen. Sin *does* exist, and all human beings are universally afflicted by it. We observe that truth every day. But scientific evidence adds nuance to how we understand our bodies and some of their struggles. So, what does this mean for Romans 5? How should we understand it? When Paul interprets Genesis 3, he affirms that all human beings are sinful. Of importance to our discussion is that Paul describes this in *typological* terms: "Death reigned from Adam to Moses, even over those whose sins were not like the transgression of Adam, who was a type [*typos*] of the one who was to come" (Rom. 5:14 RSV). As a literary device, typology conveys truth in a symbolic way. The type is like the antitype and foreshadows it, but the antitype surpasses or improves on the type. Adam is mortal and inclined toward sin.

Jesus is immortal and sinless. Biblical scholar John Walton explains this on the basis of 1 Cor. 14:45:

> Here Adam is called the "first" man, but in the context of the contrast with Christ as the "last" Adam, it cannot be seen as a claim that Adam was the first biological specimen. Since Christ was not the last biological specimen, we must instead conclude that this text is talking about the first archetype and the last archetype. . . . The biblical point is to contrast and compare Adam to Jesus and our relationship to both. Paul makes no claims about genetic relationships of all people to Adam or about material origins—only that we share the "dust" nature of the archetype.[12]

In essence, human beings are universally prone to sin, but how that relates to our bodies is complex. We should not imagine that a lone human being singlehandedly passed down (through procreation or headship) all the genetic mutations and impulses that human beings experience across the globe today. Evidence indicates that our bodies have always possessed a certain fragility and mortality inherent to original creation. Thus, wisdom invites us to be cautious about automatically assuming that a person's physical realities, including atypical sexual development, are fallen.

Evil Desire, Medical Condition, or Human Variation?

Is same-sex attraction an evil desire that springs up from a morally corrupt heart? Is it a medical condition? Or is it simply like being left-handed? Growing up, I was taught that gay people are rebellious unbelievers who make immoral choices for their lives. Conservative newsletters regularly showed up in our mailbox, warning us that gay people are sinister and bent on "recruiting" others into their depravity. The people in my Christian world never questioned the belief that gay people are morally corrupt. That made the eventual discovery of my own sexual orientation traumatic and shocking. I was the goody-two-shoes Christian who never smoked, drank, cussed, chewed, or hung around with those who did. My story is not unusual. Most gay people, especially those from Christian homes, are caught by surprise and spend years pleading with God for healing. The pain of having one's world turned upside down in this way has led some people to take their own lives. This challenges common stereotypes and a simplistic understanding of gay people as morally evil.

One possible consideration, instead of moral fallenness, is that gay people experience natural fallenness, something along the lines of a medical condition or birth defect. Some people might be reluctant to consider same-sex attraction as natural fallenness because it involves emotions and desires. A physical condition seems amoral, but impulses are closely associated with the heart and therefore character. However, this view fails to consider how the brain, which regulates sexual development and attraction, is part of our physical body. Certainly, moods and desires can stem from poor character, but they can also be neurobiological. At this point one might ask, "But isn't our whole body affected by indwelling sin anyway? Doesn't blaming biology potentially excuse any number of unintentional harmful attitudes and behaviors?"

Theologian Hans Madueme wrestles with this question and provides helpful nuance using an example of someone with Tourette's syndrome, a condition that causes uncontrolled tics that can manifest in obscene and rude language. He writes:

> What is going on in such cases? An apparent result of the fall is that people may suffer *biological* conditions that present themselves as outwardly *sinful behaviors*. Here originated sin has failed reliably to express itself in actual sins—the "sinful" behaviors are not genuinely sinful. . . . I

have genuine moral agency when my moral states and actions are properly functioning, that is, they are produced in me in a way that reliably discloses the heart—*"for out of the heart* come evil thoughts, murder, adultery, sexual immorality, theft, false testimony, slander" (Matt. 15:19 NIV). If they are produced by a more basic, overriding biological condition, then they do not reliably disclose my heart. . . . Our sins arise from "the overflow of the heart" (Matt. 12:34 NIV 1984)—the "heart" is what most fully discloses *me* (see also Gen. 6:5; Ps. 14; 58:3; Rom. 3:9–20; Mark 7:21; etc.).[13]

In the past, a child with Tourette's might have been ostracized as rebellious or demon-possessed. But it would be a mistake to characterize such a child in that way. It doesn't accurately describe what is occurring. The question, then, is how to evaluate and respond to this reality. We might view such a condition as the result of original sin and actively seek to minimize such tics. After all, obscene language can offend and hurt other people. However, such tics are not necessarily controlled by medication or treatment. Nor will prayer, repentance, or discipleship have a sanctifying effect, because the problem is not spiritual immaturity. In fact, to live in a world with people who have Tourette's, *we* have to change our posture toward them to accommodate the inevitable tics.

The scenario is similar for someone who experiences unchosen same-sex attraction. Despite therapeutic attempts, most gay people are unsuccessful in changing sexual orientation. I would like to explore how accommodation relates to gay people. But first let's look at the scientific research and its relationship to the foregoing discussion on natural fallenness. Science can help us move past stigmas and superstitions surrounding atypical sexual development.[14]

The Science of Same-Sex Attraction

Most studies indicate that gay, lesbian, and bisexual people comprise approximately 3–5 percent of the population.[15] Many of these individuals realize their sexual orientation in childhood prior to any sexual experience. A recent study of Christian college students found the average age of awareness of same-sex attraction to be eleven years old.[16] Other studies report similarly, with an average age of ten years old.[17] In other words, puberty is the pivotal starting point for many gay people's first same-sex attraction. This contrasts with stereotypes of gay and lesbian people as adults with rebellious, lewd preferences. In fact, markers of sexual orientation can occur even earlier than puberty. One strong predicator of adult same-sex attraction across cultures is childhood gender nonconformity.[18] This nonconformity is usually evident by preschool. While not all gay people are gender-nonconforming and straight people can break the mold, the research consistently shows that gay people are more likely to have had gender-atypical interests and behavior as children. As adults, gay people often continue to have cross-sex interests.

Currently, there is no scientific consensus on why people are gay or lesbian, except that this sexual orientation appears to stem from a combination of innate and environmental factors. Unfortunately, the debate on causation is highly politicized. As mentioned briefly in Chapter 1, political and religious conservatives have traditionally argued for social environmental factors in order to claim that sexual orientation is changeable. Therefore, gay and lesbian people do not need additional legal protections or rights.

Progressives also politicize their arguments, but not for the reason many conservatives assume: to justify a lustful, immoral lifestyle. Rather, for many gay people, an inborn theory simply makes sense of their lived experience. Historically, gay people have undergone (or been subjected to) all kinds of medical and psychological treatments in attempts to change their orientation without success.[19] They engage politically to help the public understand and accept that gay people do not choose their orientation. They are fighting for the chance to have life companions and families of their own without being fired from their jobs, evicted from housing, or denied service at public accommodations. They are weary of being marginalized for wanting the same basic home life that heterosexual people take for granted.

Yet, despite the way traditionalist and progressive goals influence politics, we can make some reasonable assertions about the cause of same-sex attraction. Below is a brief survey of the scientific research. (See notes for further reading.)

Social Environmental Factors

- *Disruption in parent-child relationships.* Popular among conservatives, this psychoanalytic view proposes that a child's disconnection with a same-sex parent leads to same-sex peers becoming exotic and eroticized in an attempt to repair one's gender insecurities. Most scholars in the field do not subscribe to this view because it lacks sufficient scientific evidence.[20]
- *Childhood sexual abuse.* Gay and lesbian people report higher rates of childhood sexual abuse. Studies have not proven this correlation equals causation of same-sex attraction, but if abuse does have an impact, it appears to affect males more than females.[21] The best studies suggest that 15–25 percent of gay or bisexual men experience childhood sexual abuse.[22] That means the majority, 75–85 percent of gay men, cannot attribute their sexual orientation to this etiology.
- *Natural sexual flexibility.* Bisexuality and sexual fluidity occur more frequently in women than men—although not all women experience flexibility.[23] This seems to be related, in part, to patterns of sexual arousal—for example, emotional connection for women versus erotic stimuli for men. As a result, some women may experience same-sex attraction related to relational and social dynamics.

Inborn Factors

- *Genetics.* Twin studies suggest mild genetic influence.[24] Genes do not cause a person to be gay, but genetic influences can make it more likely. A new field of study that offers additional hypotheses is epigenetics, which considers how nongenetic factors affect the way genes become active and expressed.[25] However, the research is too new to determine whether it will confirm predicted results.
- *Fraternal-birth-order effect.* In several replicated studies, males with multiple older brothers are more likely to be gay.[26] The likelihood increases 33 percent with each additional brother. A longstanding hypothesis for this is an immune response in the mother's body after repeated exposure to male fetal proteins. A recent study (2018) found that mothers with gay sons had significantly higher levels of NLGN4Y (protein) antibodies than mothers with heterosexual sons.[27] The fraternal-birth-order effect may account for up to 15–28 percent of all gay men.
- *Prenatal hormones.* One of the most compelling theoretical frameworks for causation of same-sex attraction is organizational effects of hormones in utero—that is, the relatively permanent ways the body and brain take shape at crucial stages of sexual development during pregnancy.[28] Hormones are what determine anatomical sex differences, as well as male or female typical performance. The hypothesis states that the level of exposure or response to androgens (e.g., testosterone) in utero can result in masculinization in females and demasculinization in males. The hypothesis has been confirmed in animals. In human beings, women with congenital adrenal hyperplasia (CAH), which results from high levels of androgens in utero, are more likely to be bisexual or lesbian.[29] One question scientists are still trying to sort out is why gay people don't typically experience changes to their external genitalia as do those with intersex conditions.

Another question is why CAH doesn't cause all such affected women to become gay or bisexual.

• *Brain structure.* Just as we have visible body parts that typically distinguish the sexes, so also the anatomy of the brain has regional size differences reflecting sexual differentiation caused by hormonal influences during pregnancy (see previous point). A 2016 comprehensive review of the research indicates that transgender people with early onset of gender dysphoria have characteristics of an intersex brain.[30] This finding was based on those who had not yet received any hormonal treatments to transition. Transgender people with early dysphoria are similar to those who are gay—namely, gender nonconformity in childhood and attraction to one's birth sex—raising questions about neuroanatomy in gay people.

Some research suggests gay people also have atypical brains. In one study, eighty gay and straight men and women underwent brain scans to compare regional characteristics. The study results showed gay women had less gray matter in the perirhinal cortex than straight women, and thus more closely resembled straight men, who also have less gray matter in this area.[31] In animal studies, homosexual rams have a region of the brain that is smaller (i.e., more feminized) than heterosexual rams.[32] Rams are the only mammals besides humans who demonstrate lifelong, exclusive homosexual inclinations (approximately 8 percent of the ram population).

While no factor can be pinpointed as the singular cause, much of the research indicates that prenatal influences affect development of same-sex attraction. Whether such attraction should be scientifically categorized as a medical condition and therefore natural fallenness or simply human variation is rooted in our paradigms about atypical bodies. But even if one argues for the less supported psychological etiologies, the environmental impact on a child from dysfunctional parent-child relationships or sexual abuse would still be categorized as natural fallenness—a calamity that has befallen a person rather than evidence of a morally corrupt heart. Moreover, socially induced psychological conditions can prove just as immutable as congenital conditions.

Responding to Same-Sex Attraction as Natural Fallenness

One could conclude from the scientific research that same-sex attraction is simply part of human variation. But traditionalists might still see such attraction as a birth defect or a psychological condition resulting from the fall. This raises the question, How should we respond to naturally fallen conditions? Consider an eleven-year-old boy who, because of prenatal influences, finds himself experiencing an atypical puberty. He grows up to be a gay man with the same dreams of family as his straight peers. He longs to build a home with someone. Moreover, this young man loves God and wants to live a sexually holy life, but finds lifelong celibacy unachievable. How should we respond?

In the previous two chapters, I provided reasons from Scripture and Christian tradition for considering covenanted same-sex relationships. But I suspect that some readers may have lingering hesitations in this regard stemming from discomfort with imperfection. Most Christians want to experience heaven's reality *now*. Traditionalists, in particular, want to champion the heterosexual design as the ultimate ideal without any compromise. Yet an appreciation for God's good gift of male and female can twist into an unhealthy lust for perfection. This drive goes beyond redemptive sanctifying efforts to unreasonable demands that disregard our earthly limitations. This lust for flawlessness affects not only Christians but human beings in general. We thrive on order, predictability, and conformity. Disruptions in expected patterns make us uneasy. This shows up as early as elementary school, where differences are treated with aversion. Kids mercilessly taunt "imperfections," whether speech impediments, physical disabilities, or lack of trendy clothes.

From antiquity to the present, imperfect bodies have been interpreted as a problem, a sign of sin or punishment from God (John 9:2). People with medical conditions have been exposed as infants, euthanized, hidden away, or expelled all because of a lust for perfection. Not so long ago, people suffering mental illness were chained to walls and left to lie in their own filth.[33] Sometimes people were beaten in a misguided attempt to dispel presumed demons. In Chicago, an 1881 ordinance banned people with physical disabilities from public view on grounds that they are a "disgusting object."[34] The law was not repealed until 1974.

It might seem strange to us now that such vulnerable populations would be treated poorly, but even the church has mistreated those with differences because their conditions were deemed fallen. Fortunately, changes have occurred in the last few decades that re-envision ways to respond to naturally fallen realities. Instead of exclusion or impossible standards, accommodations have been made to meet people where they are. But traditionalists have yet to offer similar accommodations to gay and lesbian people amid their plight.

In fact, prominent Christian leaders recently signed the Nashville Statement, which says that those with atypical sexual development are sinning by not maintaining a "self-conception" of a perfectly formed male or female heterosexual (Articles 5, 6, 7).[35] The preamble to the document reads, "Our true identity, as male and female persons, is given by God. It is not only foolish, but hopeless, to try to make ourselves what God did not create us to be." Astonishingly, the statement implies that gay people make themselves gay, as if it were a choice. With tragic irony, it ignores the incredible amount of pain many have suffered trying to do the opposite—make themselves heterosexual. The statement fails to help people know how to live with the actual bodies they have.

So, what is a helpful response? What does accommodation look like for gay people living with this unchosen reality? Covenant relationships can provide an essential source of companionship and support. Some argue that we should not allow such relationships any more than we would permit other sinful habits. Same-sex attraction is often compared with alcoholism or gluttony. But this is largely based on a fundamental misunderstanding of gay people. Same-sex attraction is not an addiction or an excess of desire. Alcoholism is a compulsion that significantly impairs relationships and life functioning. Gluttony causes health problems because of its excess. In contrast, covenanted same-sex relationships can be life-giving.

Same-sex attraction is the same as heterosexual attraction—the familial drive that makes us want to couple with another person and build a home. Same-sex relationships are equally capable of exhibiting the fruit of the Spirit as straight ones. In fact, mandating lifelong celibacy or encouraging heterosexual marriages for gay people is often what has caused significant harm, not covenanted same-sex relationships. Traditionalists have an opportunity to make a positive difference in the lives of gay and lesbian people by re-envisioning possibilities for a redemptive response. Thus far, perfectionism has been an obstacle to considering life-giving options.

Human Variation: The Gift of Difference

A strong case can be made for allowing covenanted same-sex relationships as an accommodation for a naturally fallen condition, but we might also consider that being gay is simply part of human variation. What if gay people are attracted to the same sex for similar reasons that a small percentage of people have turned out left-handed? Most people in the West today realize there is nothing wrong with being left-handed. But that hasn't always been the case. Left-handers, who comprise around 10 percent of the global population, have long been stigmatized. In many cultures, the word "left" still has a sinister connotation.

In 1946 Abram Blau, the former chief psychiatrist of the New York City Board of Education, counseled that left-handed children should be forced to use their right hand lest they develop severe cognitive disorders.[36] Sometimes children had their left hands tied behind their backs or were humiliated and punished for using the left hand. One study by psychologist Clare Porac indicates that efforts to force right-handedness were common in Canada until the 1980s. In many countries around the world today, left-handers continue to face discrimination. Much of this over-the-top reaction is for no other reason than that left-handedness happens to be different than the norm.

Human beings appear to have an innate desire for sameness. Studies show we are attracted to people who look similar to us.[37] We gravitate toward those who have the same opinions and interests. Studies also show that our beliefs are not formulated by facts as much as by desire to blend into a social group.[38] Most of us will hide or minimize differences to avoid jeopardizing our insider status.[39]

Fear of losing our place of belonging is a primary motivation for our reaction to difference. When something unusual appears on the scene, we naturally want to protect our group's cohesion and equilibrium. This leads to targeting almost any difference for expulsion or forced conformity, even if it poses no real harm, as with people who are left-handed. If people the world over have been alarmed by left-handers to the point of "fixing" them, how much more severely will people react to those who are gay?

Our discomfort with difference can lead us to misdiagnose and mistreat human variation as illness or fallenness.[40] But there is another way to think about difference. The early church father Augustine also wrestled with whether to diagnose rare phenomena as fallen or God-created. In the case of intersex people, he concluded they are not a product of the fall.[41] God intentionally created a sexual minority outside the binary. In *City of God* he writes:

> For God is the Creator of all things: He Himself knows
> where and when anything should be, or should have been,
> created; and He knows how to weave the beauty of the
> whole out of the similarity and diversity of its parts. The

man who cannot view the whole is offended by what he takes to be the deformity of a part; but this is because he does not know how it is to be adapted or related to the whole. . . . God forbid, however, that someone who does not know why the Creator has done what He has done should be foolish enough to suppose that God has in such cases erred.[42]

Augustine came to this remarkable conclusion without the benefit of modern scientific tools. If his assessment of visible differences in sexual development led him to this view, one can't help but wonder how he might have responded to knowledge of neuroanatomy and other invisible inborn characteristics. Given our increased scientific insight, we might consider how Augustine's view applies to gay and lesbian people. Instead of treating same-sex attraction as a symptom of moral corruption or even natural fallenness, we can appreciate it as diversity within the whole.[43]

Summing It Up

Christians often consider same-sex attraction an outcome of the fall, whether moral or natural fallenness. In this chapter, we explored how science helps us contemplate what that means on a practical level. Evidence indicates our bodily conditions and impulses were not passed down by a lone *Homo sapiens*. Similarly, mortality and physical fragility existed prior to any fall. Wisdom invites us to be cautious about assuming that all bodily realities are the result of original sin.

We also examined three possibilities for categorizing same-sex attraction: moral fallenness, natural fallenness, and human variation. Science provides good evidence for considering same-sex attraction as either natural fallenness or human variation. In the case of natural fallenness, I encouraged traditionalists to re-envision redemptive responses to congenital conditions. Existing approaches that counsel mandatory lifelong celibacy or heterosexual marriage for gay people can cause harm.

Finally, we considered the possibility of understanding same-sex attraction as human variation that is not fallen. Scientific advancements have given us greater knowledge of sexual development. Just as we no longer try to "fix" left-handed people, we need not impose unnecessary treatments and restrictions on gay and lesbian people.

FURTHER READING

J. Michael Bailey et al. "Sexual Orientation, Controversy, and Science." *Psychological Science in the Public Interest* 17 (2016): 45–101.

John Bimson. "Doctrines of the Fall and Sin after Darwin." In *Theology after Darwin*, ed. Michael S. Northcott and R. J. Berry, 106–22. Milton Keynes: Paternoster, 2009.

Brian Brock. "Augustine's Hierarchies of Human Wholeness and Their Healing." In *Disability in the Christian Tradition: A Reader*, ed. Brian Brock and John Swinton, 65–100. Grand Rapids: Eerdmans, 2012.

Peter Enns. *The Evolution of Adam: What the Bible Does and Doesn't Say about Human Origins.* Grand Rapids: Brazos, 2012.

Hans Madueme. "'The Most Vulnerable Part of the Whole Christian Account': Original Sin and Modern Science." In *Adam, the Fall, and Original Sin: Theological, Biblical, and Scientific Perspectives*, ed. Hans Madueme and Michael Reeves, 225–50. Grand Rapids: Baker Academic, 2014.

Scot McKnight and Dennis R. Venema. *Adam and the Genome: Reading Scripture after Genetic Science.* Grand Rapids: Brazos, 2017.

John H. Walton. *The Lost World of Genesis One: Ancient Cosmology and the Origins Debate.* Downers Grove, IL: InterVarsity Press, 2009.

8

Imagining a New Response
to the Gay and Lesbian Community

This book began with a glance back at the church's historical response to gay and lesbian people. As new knowledge has surfaced, reactions have shifted. Early responses assumed harsh caricatures of gay people as spiritually depraved, criminal, or mentally disturbed. As more Christians came to know ordinary gay people (often friends and family), these negative caricatures were challenged. The church began to acknowledge that same-sex attraction is unchosen, often shows up during puberty, and does not change for the majority of gay people. Moreover, as gay Christians have braved coming out of the closet, evidence of their spiritual devotion has countered previous stereotypes of godlessness.

With each new insight, the church has striven to respond with greater integrity. Instead of criminalizing gay people, the church made efforts to heal same-sex attraction. Prayer, therapy, and support groups promised to resolve the childhood wounds that allegedly caused same-sex attraction. However, it eventually became clear that spiritual and therapeutic methods were not successful in changing most people's sexual orientation. This realization led many traditionalists to shift from trying to cure gay people to advocating lifelong celibacy. Now the church finds itself at yet another crossroad.

In the preceding pages, I have provided evidence to support a shift to acceptance of same-sex relationships. In addition to key arguments on complementarity in Chapter 3 that ground marriage in covenant fidelity (not sexual differentiation), I have offered four main arguments related to Scripture and ethics, the feasibility of celibacy, and how we conceptualize the fall in light of scientific evidence. These areas need greater attention in the current debate:

1. *Proper interpretation of Scripture requires recognizing the overarching intent of biblical mandates, namely, a good and just world.* In ancient Israel, holding a rapist accountable and protecting the victim looked different than it does in the church today. That is because we have imagined possibilities for fulfilling the intent of the rape law other than requiring a victim to marry her perpetrator. By doing so, we have *enhanced*, not discarded, the purpose of the original law. In the same way, we will benefit from discerning the overarching intent of sexual laws in Scripture to determine how they might be fulfilled and enhanced for gay people in ways not currently imagined by the traditionalist position.

2. *Scripture itself teaches us that biblical mandates, including creation ordinances, cannot be applied without a deliberative process.* To flatly apply law across the board without discernment for individual cases is a misuse of Scripture. Traditionalists have generally viewed the deliberative process as a general one: Are same-sex relationships collectively right or wrong? But the biblical authors demonstrate that even laws that prohibit something cannot be blindly applied. Discernment is still required on a case-by-case basis. Among key criteria for the deliberative process is attention to human need. Jesus and the biblical authors applied humanitarian exceptions to the rule.

   Scripture also provides examples of case law (e.g., Deut. on slavery). Many conservative churches today recognize the need for casuistry to respond to ethical concerns not directly

addressed in the Bible. In contrast to the humanitarian exception to the rule, a determination from case law may extrapolate
an overarching principle that can be applied broadly rather
than only on a case-by-case basis (e.g., Focus on the Family's
allowance of anyone divorced prior to conversion to remarry).

3. *Evidence indicates that lifelong celibacy is not achievable for
every person.* Lifelong celibacy is possible for some, but traditionalists have not demonstrated that it is possible for every
person. Christian tradition, social scientific studies, and even
the writings of conservatives all agree that lifelong celibacy is
not realistic for most people.[1] My hope is that traditionalists
will openly and honestly wrestle with this reality.

4. *Evidence shows same-sex attraction is not moral fallenness; it
could be understood as natural fallenness or human variation.*
The conversation will benefit from unpacking the abstract
concept of the fall in light of scientific evidence. This includes
consideration of accommodation for congenital conditions in
a way that helps people navigate life with the bodies they have,
not "idealistic" ones they don't have. We can also consider that
same-sex attraction is not fallen at all, but a rare variation that
has been unnecessarily shunned.

In essence, accepting same-sex relationships does not require
compromising Scripture. To the contrary, taking Scripture *more* seriously teaches us to apply these texts in a way the biblical authors
themselves model. Scripture also helps us navigate the physical
world. Bringing the Bible and science into conversation with each
other enriches our understanding of both. Together they enable us
to discern truth about our bodies and the best way to fulfill God's
intentions for humanity.

How Might a Traditionalist Respond Now?

The possibility of accepting same-sex relationships naturally raises the question of what that might require practically. Many traditionalists worry that accepting gay couples would demand giving up God's design of male and female. But supporting covenanted same-sex relationships in no way discounts the beauty of male-female complementarity. Traditionalists are right to say there is something incredibly meaningful about what women bring to the world as women and what men bring to the world as men. While some voices argue for same-sex relationships by deconstructing sex and gender, such efforts are a well-meaning but misguided method of countering discrimination (à la the "love is color-blind" fallacy).[2] We can affirm the reality that most people are born heterosexual males and females *and* acknowledge that people can experience other types of sexual development.

Recognizing the supportive benefit of covenanted relationships for gay people in no way diminishes or threatens heterosexual relationships. In fact, the sexual and relational problems we see in Western culture today are the result of de-emphasizing covenant. Promiscuity, sexually transmitted diseases, sex-trafficking, and divorce all primarily result from disregard for covenant. Rather than fighting against marriage for gay people, traditionalists can affirm family values and *enhance* respect for covenant by including same-sex couples.

Theologically, acceptance of same-sex relationships can be understood in different ways. Three possible options are the traditionalist exception view, the traditionalist case-law view, and the affirming view.

- The *traditionalist exception view* ordinarily considers same-sex relationships morally wrong but applies a humanitarian exception to the rule for those unable to achieve celibacy. A covenant relationship is considered less problematic than promiscuity.

Allowance is given on a case-by-case basis depending on the spiritual needs of the individuals involved. Bisexual people would be encouraged toward heterosexual marriage. Same-sex relationships might be labeled as "partnerships" rather than "marriages" if marriage is doctrinally defined as requiring pro-creative potential.[3]

Progressives may find this view unsatisfying. A potential problem is that the local church community that allows this exception will be tempted to treat the relationship as second class, making it difficult to enthusiastically support a couple in building a strong, healthy partnership. Yet the exception view can still have value for gay and lesbian people who cognitively struggle to arrive at an affirming position, yet are unable to achieve celibacy. It provides a means out of the psychologically and spiritually debilitating double-bind.

- The *traditionalist case-law view* considers male-female com-plementarity God's design for marriage but acknowledges that Paul never addresses the ethical dilemma of gay and lesbian people who are unable to achieve life-long celibacy. By casu-istically applying Paul's instruction of marriage for those with strong passions, the traditionalist case-law view considers cov-enanted same-sex relationships morally acceptable. This might be understood as a humanitarian exception to the rule. But it could also be applied comprehensively to all gay and lesbian people in congruence with Martin Luther's conclusion that most people require marriage to thrive spiritually.

Whether or not bisexual people might consider a same-sex partner within this view depends on the deliberative pro-cess. In general, heterosexual marriage would be encouraged when possible, but this could be evaluated on a case-by-case basis (e.g., a bisexual person might be the most suitable part-ner given important factors like shared faith and values). The traditionalist case-law view also allows flexibility for labeling a same-sex relationship as marriage.

• The *affirming view* acknowledges the goodness of male and female complementarity but doesn't consider it a mandate for marriage. Gay and lesbian people represent meaningful and good human variation. Being gay (or bisexual) is not a fallen condition; it is part of the whole of God's creation. The affirming view believes same-sex relationships can meet Scripture's foundational criterion of marriage: covenant fidelity.

The affirming view is based on two proposals. First, the biblical prohibitions are deemed prescientific in the same way biblical cosmology is prescientific. Paul's concern for what is "unnatural" must be understood in his historical context. In Jewish and Greco-Roman sources, "unnatural" expressed concern for non-procreative sex and violation of gender norms that placed women in a lower status than men. Paul was also influenced by Stoicism's concept of a rational universe and seemed to believe that all people are heterosexual. In his view, desire for the same sex results from excessive lust after a person turns away from God. He did not have advanced technology to help him understand the internal processes of sexual development, including prenatal factors.

Second, the affirming view can be based on the overarching intent of the sexual laws in Scripture. If the purpose of the sexual laws is to promote a just world where people do not mistreat each other, it can be argued that same-sex covenanted relationships meet that criteria. For example, adultery involves betrayal, and incest creates problematic power dynamics within a family (and tries to create kin with someone already kin). Thus, these biblical prohibitions are still necessary to prevent abuse. But same-sex relationships are not harmful by virtue of their same-sex nature. Just as we have enhanced the intention of the biblical laws on rape to better support women, we can improve upon sexual ethics for people who experience same-sex attraction. The affirming view values the intent of the biblical sexual laws but envisions more possibilities for fulfilling that purpose.

What Does Acceptance Mean for Gay and Lesbian People?

Just as there are theological options in accepting same-sex relationships, there is flexibility in people's decisions for their lives. Coming to an affirming position does not mean treating marriage as superior to celibacy. Celibacy is a valuable vocation in its own right. Every person, gay or straight, must seek God for direction. There are good reasons to pursue a celibate life, including serving God with greater freedom. Either way, whether celibate or married, all people need support from friends, family, and spiritual care providers.

The culture war often makes it difficult for gay and lesbian people to discern a vocation to either celibacy or partnership. Gay people have been used as pawns by both sides of the debate. Extreme pressure is often exerted to force gay people to believe or behave in ways that comply with a given community's expectations. While churches or political groups naturally have guidelines for group participation, when acceptance is contingent on conformity, this can cause harmful psychological distress for the gay person.

Being gay is not easy. Being gay *and* Christian can be even harder as one wrestles with opposing theological views and politicization around the issue. Ultimately, coercion is not effective. The only way gay and lesbian people can live healthy spiritual lives is to come to peace with their own decisions. The best thing that traditionalists and progressives can do is to walk alongside each person with reassurances of God's unconditional love. Paradoxically, it is freedom that allows us to hear and surrender to the will of God.

A supportive church community is crucial for gay and lesbian people who feel invited by God into marriage. Robust encouragement will undergird vows of fidelity in sickness and in health. Treating these relationships as somehow tainted makes people's pursuit of faithfulness and holiness much more difficult. I hope the church will nurture these covenant bonds to make them strong. More than that, I hope gay and lesbian couples will be a source of edification to straight people as imitators of Christ's love for the church. The world needs more people who model Jesus's promise "I will never leave you nor forsake you."

Tying the Threads Together:
My Personal Journey to Acceptance

While I hope this book will help traditionalists feel more confident in accepting same-sex relationships, I also know from personal experience that this kind of shift is a challenging step to take. My own journey to acceptance took more than twenty years. As a way to close this book and tie together its many threads, I would like to share that story with you now. I offer it as encouragement to anyone who is considering a shift but is uncertain what that might look like.

My journey began when my parents initiated me into our small-town conservative Baptist church just weeks after my birth. From then on, it was church at least three times a week. I enjoyed all the blessings of a faith community: Sunday school, singing in rest homes with the children's choir, Pioneer Girls, youth group, mission trips, and more. The church raised me and, in many ways, nurtured my soul. But when it came to learning about gay people, my church and the broader conservative Christian world could take me only as far as its own perceptions.

As the church moved through its own shifts and stages, I journeyed alongside it. I started out with negative stereotypes before arriving at more nuanced conclusions. My images of gay people were formed by whispered stories, conservative newsletters, and political rants about the "gay agenda." I pictured gay people as weird deviants who acted as they did out of spiritual complacency. Notably, my views were not shaped by any personal experiences with gay people. And it never occurred to me to question the accuracy of the messages I heard.

It was only when I realized that I am gay that I confronted the contradiction between the church's stories and my own life. Coming to terms with my sexuality was traumatic. I never imagined that I could be gay. Gay people were atheists and backsliders. I was the good Christian girl who dreamed of serving Christ as a missionary. Falling in love with my best friend, who I had met at a Christian camp in my late teens, threw my world upside down.

At the time, I didn't really know what it meant to be gay. I assumed it was a difficult phase that would pass with enough prayer. I spent hours in the library at my Baptist college, combing through the Bible and commentaries to see what Scripture had to say. My studies confirmed what I already believed: every reference prohibited same-sex relationships. Despite distress and confusion about my predicament, I remained earnest in my commitment to obey God.

I sought help from a counselor at my school who referred me to an ex-gay ministry. There I met other Christians who shared my experience and understood what I was going through. It gave me hope that I could soon put this problem behind me. I fully embraced the ex-gay philosophy of sexual orientation change. For two years I diligently engaged the curriculum, addressing perceived childhood wounds and embracing my femininity. I prayed and practiced spiritual disciplines. I confessed sexual sin to leaders. I faithfully attended the support groups and traveled to Exodus conferences. But after the program was complete, my attractions remained unchanged.

I persisted in my efforts, believing patience was the answer, but eventually the lack of success led to increasing depression. For my own sanity, I got off the ex-gay treadmill and resigned myself to lifelong celibacy. Except the heart never really resigns itself to loneliness. I didn't realize how much I was still holding out hope until several years later when Yarhouse and Jones published their ex-gay study, and my heart sank.[4] They had attempted to refute activist claims that sexual orientation change is impossible, but the results were not promising. I remember the day: September 19, 2007. In a blog post, I wrote:

I knew the study results were coming. I was waiting for the announcement and thought it would make for an interesting conversation. What I didn't expect was to feel sad. While everyone else seems to be either refuting the findings ("Gays can't change!") or championing the results ("Gays can change!"), my first reaction was: *Fifteen percent conversion? Is that all?*[5] I know not everyone changes. That is nothing new to me or those involved in ex-gay ministry. But, something about these statistics drew a line I would rather not see—those who change to heterosexual attraction/functioning are a small minority. Smaller than many of us care to admit.

I had hoped the conversion rate would be higher. Maybe then I wouldn't be single. Like the 23% in the study, I am leading a well-adjusted celibate life. . . . Yet, chastity is a bittersweet success. Deep in the heart of every ex-gay ministry participant is the longing for intimacy with another. We work the program in hopes of, not only attaining chastity, but also finding the key that unlocks the door to a God-blessed union.[6]

The mantra in ex-gay ministry was "Our goal is not heterosexuality; it's holiness." But the movement was double-minded. Yes, the goal was holiness, but we also strove for healing. We believed all things are possible in Christ. Ex-gay newsletters and conferences frequently highlighted success stories of formerly gay people now heterosexually married with children. But, as time eventually revealed, that optimism often masked failed marriages and lack of orientation change. The Yarhouse and Jones study confirmed for me what I already experienced in my own life and what I saw among other ex-gay ministry participants: most gay people do not experience sexual orientation change.

When I came to terms with the truth about conversion rates, I remained committed to celibacy. I didn't want to be like other ex-gays who ended up embracing same-sex relationships. I observed how they revised their theology when attempts to change did not succeed. In my mind they were selling out. They put their sexuality before God. I wanted Christ to be first in my life no matter what the cost. I soon became an advocate of the celibate gay movement. My journey might have ended there, where many traditionalists today have also landed. But new questions kept popping up that would not give me rest.

After seminary, I went on to study the Bible full-time in post-graduate work. The deeper I engaged Scripture, the more I encountered unturned stones. To address my questions, I pulled together a discernment group. I knew any changes in my beliefs needed to happen within Christian community. The group consisted of thirteen people across the United States, most of them pastors or theologians, including well-known people in the church's discussion on sexuality. It was a mix of traditionalists and progressives. I chose them for their spiritual maturity and knowledge of the subject. For two months we engaged in conversation through video chats, a private social-media group, emails, and phone calls. I pulled out all the stops in wrestling with hard questions, trying to discern what God was telling me.

The end results surprised me. Rather than a black-and-white answer, I heard God saying "freedom." Not the kind of freedom that celebrates licentiousness, but the kind of freedom that loves you no matter what, even when you don't measure up. I still discerned that male and female is God's good design, but alongside that now stood recognition of human limitations. I sensed God's acknowledgment that not all people can attain lifelong celibacy. I also sensed more clearly than ever how much God created human beings with a deep need for family, for rootedness. We are not designed for living alone or with serial roommates—the unfortunate lot of most single people in the West. Everyone needs covenant and kinship.

Having my needs for kinship validated was encouraging, but true to my spiritual zeal, I determined to be strong enough not to need an accommodation. I would persist in the celibate life and meet my needs for kinship through intentional community. Theologically,

I believed God was merciful toward those unable to achieve lifelong celibacy. But personally, I would remain committed to unmarried life. With those conclusions drawn, I thought I could finally close the book on all my questions and move on with life.

My peace lasted but a few weeks. I had this nagging feeling that something was unresolved. With no interest in rehashing the issue, I ignored it. Hadn't I worked through all the questions already? For three years, I avoided facing the feelings head-on. During that season, I worked part-time as a spiritual care provider. One word of encouragement I often gave people is that sometimes turbulence means the Holy Spirit is about to give birth to something. We can mistake the unrest as something negative, but what if we embrace the labor, anticipating God's movement? Eventually, I swallowed my own words. And the result is this book.

These chapters represent my spiritual and intellectual journey through Scripture, Christian tradition, theology, and science to find answers on same-sex relationships. Unlike most arguments that make a case for same-sex relationships, I do not seek to overturn much of the truth of traditionalist theology. When I consider the views that I held as a traditionalist, I can still say "Amen!" I still affirm God's good creation of male and female complementarity. My response to traditionalists is not "No, you are wrong" or even "Yes, but." My reply is "Yes, *and.*"

I came to a greater understanding of how biblical mandates function. I learned that laws in and of themselves do not automatically fulfill the will of God. Biblical mandates are only meaningful in their particularities if they achieve the purpose to which they point: love of God and neighbor. I also learned that the biblical authors and Jesus did not blindly apply mandates. They engaged in a deliberative process even for creation ordinances. They affirmed the truth of creation ordinances like Sabbath *and* made room for cases that didn't fit the box. Moreover, I saw how conservative churches regularly apply biblical case law to difficult ethical questions, yet neglect to do so for gay and lesbian people.

I also explored the question of celibacy. I came to greater appreciation that no evidence exists that it's possible for all people. I saw that setting a bar that cannot be reached renders the mandate meaningless and perpetuates spiritual and psychological trauma for the person trapped in that impossible situation. I came to realize that covenant relationships, rather than lowering the bar, were the very thing that could help gay people live holy and fruitful lives.

Finally, I pondered the fall in light of science and considered how same-sex attraction might be accurately conceptualized. It made sense to me that if same-sex attraction is a congenital or medical condition, a redemptive accommodation is a Spirit-led option. At the same time, I saw how scientific evidence opens the door to viewing gay people as part of God's good creation. As Augustine concluded, just because something is atypical doesn't mean it's fallen.

So, where does that leave me now in my own life? Ever since I was a child, I have felt an insistent call to serve God. Many times, I asked God to let me be a floor sweeper in the Kingdom if that meant I could work by my Creator's side. That feeling has never left me. God means more to me than anything. God is the reason I get up in the morning. That reality has also shaped the way I view marriage. When I was young, I often prayed for a spouse who loved Jesus as much as I do. I dreamed of what we could do together for Christ when holding up each other's arms. But over time, I stopped saying that prayer. I thought being gay meant it wasn't something I could have. My heart has never stopped longing for that person, though. And now I find myself whispering that prayer again.

Summing It Up

The topic of same-sex relationships provokes all manner of arguments and emotions. Understandably so. Christians on both sides of the debate have strong positions because we care about the gospel vision in which all things are reconciled in God and shalom reigns.

We can find encouragement in the fact that we are not the first to wrestle with important doctrines. The creedal debates that parsed out Christ's divinity and humanity were arguably more crucial and central. The leaders in those debates also experienced their fair share of stress and urgency. Throughout Christian tradition, every generation has faced significant theological challenges. We are in good company.

The current conversation on same-sex relationships has largely reached an impasse. In this book, I have pushed essential issues to the forefront that I believe are being overlooked. These include attending to the overarching intent of biblical mandates, engaging in a deliberative process for creation ordinances, discussing honestly the feasibility of celibacy, and reflecting on the fall in light of science. I have also discussed theological options for accepting same-sex relationships.

I firmly believe it is possible to imagine a new response to the gay community—and to do so with faithfulness to God's Word. In fact, this journey has proven to me the depth of Scripture and its ability to speak into our greatest life challenges. I offer my conclusions as possibilities to ponder, and I welcome you to dialogue with me. As we continue the conversation, may God grant us wisdom, grace, and charity.

Notes

Note to the Preface

*Unless otherwise indicated, all the biblical quotations in this book are taken from the NIV.

Notes to Chapter 1

1. I intentionally use "gay and lesbian" more often in this book than "LGBT." I also use "gay" as inclusive of all people who are predominantly attracted to the same sex, regardless of gender. This book focuses particularly on people who do not experience bisexuality or fluidity in their sexual orientation and thus are forced to make life decisions that are different from those who are able to function in a heterosexual relationship. Similarly, the church's response to transgender people is distinct, and the issues in that conversation are different than those for gay people. I do not presume to speak for transgender people. Finally, I avoid the term "queer" because this is a word that conservative audiences are not likely to understand. It can also be a triggering word for some gay and lesbian people.

2. In his books *Same-Sex Unions in Pre-Modern Europe* and *Christianity, Social Tolerance, and Homosexuality*, John Boswell claims same-sex marriage was accepted by the church at various times in history. However, his scholarship is problematic. Most scholars reject his argument as flawed.

3. Chrysostom, *Homily 4 on Romans*. Translation from Gerald L. Bray, ed., *Romans*, Ancient Christian Commentary on Scripture, New Testament IV (Downers Grove, IL: InterVarsity Press, 1998), 45.

4. Chrysostom, *Homily 4 on Romans*, 46.

5. Ewald Marting Plass, *What Luther Says: An Anthology*, vol. 1 (Saint Louis: Concordia, 1959), 134.

6. Matthew Henry, "Leviticus 18" and "Leviticus 20," in *Matthew Henry's Commentary on the Whole Bible*, vol. 1, https://www.blueletterbible.org/Comm/ mhc/Lev/Lev_018.cfm, https://www.blueletterbible.org/Comm/mhc/Lev/Lev _020.cfm.

7. For more on ancient inborn or medical explanations for same-sex attraction, see Bernadette J. Brooten, *Love Between Women: Early Christian Responses to Female Homoeroticism* (Chicago: University of Chicago Press, 1996), 115–73.

8. Philo, *On the Contemplative Life* 63. See the discussion in William Loader, *Philo, Josephus, and the Testaments on Sexuality: Attitudes towards Sexuality in the Writings of Philo and Josephus and in the Testaments of the Twelve Patriarchs* (Grand Rapids: Eerdmans, 2011), 211.

9. Brooten, *Love Between Women*, 321–22.

10. Brooten, *Love Between Women*, 336.

11. Brooten, *Love Between Women*, 119.

12. The medical theories were also rooted in ideas of masculinity such that the male penetrator was not considered as diseased as the passive male partner. Both partners in a lesbian relationship were considered unhealthy because such a relationship circumvented procreation and submission to a man. In the *Apocalypse of Peter*, passive males and both female partners are depicted in hell, but not the active male partner. See Brooten, *Love Between Women*, 307.

13. The existence of medical hypotheses in antiquity is important for the present discussion on the church's response to gay and lesbian people. Recently, several commentators, drawing on philosopher Michel Foucault, have suggested that sexual orientation is a modern invention. It developed after Freud categorized sexual acts, turning them into psychological diagnoses. These diagnoses, in turn, became identities. Traditionalists who believe that sexual orientation is an invention argue that there is no such thing as a gay person; sexual orientation is socially constructed. As a construct, they suggest, same-sex attraction is changeable and can be remedied with spiritual discipline. However, awareness of sexual orientation—in the sense of inborn, persistent attractions—existed in antiquity long before Freud. For more on this, see Brooten, *Love Between Women*, 143–73; and Jesi Egans, "Abusing Foucault: How Conservatives and Liberals Misunderstand 'Social Construct' Sexuality," *Slate*, March 4, 2014, http:// www.slate.com/blogs/outward/2014/03/04/sexuality_as_social_construct_fou cault_is_misunderstood_by_conservatives.html.

14. Eugen Steinach attempted to treat perceived hormonal disorder by transplanting the testicles of a straight man onto the testicles of a gay man. See Thomas Schlich, *The Origins of Organ Transplantation: Surgery and Laboratory Science, 1880–1930* (Rochester, NY: University of Rochester Press, 2010), 112.

15. Evelyn Hooker, "The Adjustment of the Male Overt Homosexual," *Journal of Projective Techniques* 21 (1957): 18–31. Notably, this evidence was apparent long before gay activists urged the mental health profession to remove homosexuality from the Diagnostic and Statistical Manual of Mental Disorders.

16. C. S. Lewis is quoted in Sheldon Vanauken, *A Severe Mercy* (New York: Harper & Row, 1977), 146–48.

17. However, Metropolitan Community Church, founded by and for LGBT people, was established in 1968.

18. James White and Jeffrey D. Niell, *The Same Sex Controversy: Defending and Clarifying the Bible's Message about Homosexuality* (Minneapolis: Bethany House, 2002), 17.

19. Alan Sears and Craig Osten, *The Homosexual Agenda: Exposing the Principal Threat to Religious Freedom Today* (Nashville: Broadman & Holman, 2003), 19.

20. Michael Pakaluk, "Homosexuality and the Principle of Nondiscrimination," in *Same-Sex Matters: The Challenge of Homosexuality*, ed. Christopher Wolfe (Dallas: Spence, 2000), 76.

21. Scott Lively writes: "It is not mere coincidence that the emperors of Rome in its horrific final days were homosexual; that Adolf Hitler's inner circle were mostly homosexual; and that nearly all of the most prolific serial killers in U.S. history were homosexual. It is not mere coincidence that America's cultural decline parallels the rise of 'gay rights'" (see "Agents of the Death Agenda," *Life Advocate*, May 1996).

22. Joseph Nicolosi, "The Gay Deception," in *Homosexuality and American Public Life*, ed. Christopher Wolfe (Dallas: Spence, 1999), 105.

23. Nicolosi, "The Gay Deception," 105.

24. Michael Pakaluk, "Homosexuality and the Common Good," in *Homosexuality and American Public Life*, ed. Wolfe, 181.

25. In 2003 the U.S. Supreme Court ruled in *Lawrence v. Texas* to strike down anti-sodomy laws in the fourteen states that still had them.

26. My discussion of the "conservative church" particularly addresses evangelicals. However, there is overlap with other traditions. For example, the ex-gay movement also involved Mormons (Evergreen), Jews (JONAH), and Catholics (Courage, as well as Joseph Nicolosi). One primary distinction is that Catholics tend to be much more affirming of celibacy and the reality that sexual orientation is not likely to change (Nicolosi excepted).

27. Tanya Erzen, *Straight to Jesus: Sexual and Christian Conversions in the Ex-Gay Movement* (Berkeley: University of California Press, 2006), 32.

28. Jeff Konrad, *You Don't Have to Be Gay* (Newport Beach: Pacific, 2000), 9–10. First printing in 1987.

29. Erzen, *Straight to Jesus*, 40.

30. The 2007 movie *Save Me* stars Chad Allen as Mark, a gay drug addict who enters an ex-gay program. The film is directed by Robert Cary.

31. The celibate gay Christian movement also finds seeds in ex-gays who were disillusioned with ex-gay ideology and had been critiquing it from the inside for years (e.g., challenging Alan Chambers to acknowledge lack of sexual orientation change and objecting to his collaboration with Religious Right politics, etc.). A small dissenting group of ex-gays began privately communicating and brainstorming a new movement around 2008. Shortly thereafter, evangelical Wesley Hill, who had never been involved in the ex-gay movement, discussed the reality of unchanged attractions in his book *Washed and Waiting* (2010). This was the first evangelical book that frankly discussed lack of sexual orientation change. Some folk from the dissenting group of ex-gays connected with Hill. Eventually, in August 2011, Hill and Ron Belgau started a private blog, *De Spirituali Amicitia* (spiritual friendship). This private community grew substantially, especially drawing young men in their twenties. A public version of the blog went live in April 2012 as *Spiritual Friendship* (spiritualfriendship.org). Significantly, this new movement is characterized by a strong ecumenical relationship between Catholics and evangelicals, as well as by its youthfulness.

32. Warren Throckmorton, "Alan Chambers: 99.9% Have Not Experienced a Change in Their Orientation," personal blog, January 9, 2012, http://www.wthrockmorton.com/2012/01/09/alan-chambers-99-9-have-not-experienced-a-change-in-their-orientation/.

33. Lou Chibarro Jr., "Former 'Ex-Gay' Leader to March in Pride Parade," *Washington Blade*, January 9, 2016, http://www.washingtonblade.com/2016/06/09/former-ex-gay-leader-to-march-in-pride-parade/.

34. I discuss research on sexual orientation change in Chapter 6.

35. Julie Rodgers, a young ex-gay who switched to the celibate gay movement around 2013, became a prominent voice for the movement before changing her views to affirming in 2015.

36. A friend of this movement is Dr. Mark Yarhouse, professor at Regent University, who oversees the Institute for the Study of Sexual Identity.

37. Another excellent book related to celibate gays is Tim Otto's *Oriented to Faith: Transforming the Conflict over Gay Relationships* (Eugene, OR: Cascade Books, 2014). However, unlike Wesley Hill, Otto made a vow of celibacy for vocational reasons and not because of objections to same-sex relationships. His book presents both sides of the debate interspersed with his personal life stories and perspectives as a celibate gay person.

38. By Progressive Christian theology, I mean primarily views on Scripture and non-marital sex. For example, one keynote speaker at the 2018 conference, Dr. Yvette Flunder, stated "I am a Bible" to emphasize that God is still speaking to people. Most evangelicals would be uncomfortable with that statement. At the same time, GCN/QCF has allowed celibate gay people to lead break-out sessions/workshops. Similarly, some affirming LGBTQ Christians at GCN/QCF hold an evangelical view of Scripture's authority, as well as believe that sex should occur in the context of a lifelong covenant.

Notes to Chapter 2

1. When discussing the biblical authors in their ancient setting, I use the vocabulary "same-sex relations," "male-male sexual intercourse," "female-female sexual intercourse," "homoeroticism," and "pederasty" (if that is specifically called for). "Homosexuality" is a modern term, as is "gay," "lesbian," or "queer." The phrase "same-sex relationships" is also more appropriate to our context since it implies consensual, committed relationships. In reference to our context, these terms are acceptable, but they are not accurate labels to use when describing homoeroticism in antiquity. That is not because people with exclusive attractions to the same sex didn't exist or because some peer relationships never occurred, but because homoeroticism was understood and performed differently in the past than today.

2. Marc Brettler, *How to Read the Bible* (Philadelphia: Jewish Publication Society, 2010).

3. There is no evidence for widespread fertility cults or temple prostitution in the ancient Near East or Israel. This notion was popularized, in part, by the debunked work of myth-ritual theorist Sir James Frazer, as found in his book *The Golden Bough*. Various scholars have addressed the lack of evidence. For a start, check out S. M. Baugh, "Cult Prostitution in New Testament Ephesus: A Reappraisal," *Journal of the Evangelical Theological Society* 42 (1999): 443–60; Stephanie L. Budin, "Sacred Prostitution in the First Person," in *Prostitutes and Courtesans in the Ancient World*, ed. Christopher A. Faraone and Laura K. McClure (Madison: University of Wisconsin Press, 2006), 77–92; Martha Roth, "Marriage, Divorce, and the Prostitute in Ancient Mesopotamia," in Faraone and McClure, *Prostitutes and Courtesans*, 21–39; Joan Goodnick Westenholz, "Tamar, Qĕdēšā, Qadištu, and Sacred Prostitutes in Mesopotamia," *Harvard Theological Review* 82 (1989): 245–65. For a rebuttal, see John Day, "Does the Old Testament Refer to Sacred Prostitution and Did It Actually Exist in Ancient Israel?," in *Biblical and Near Eastern Essays*, ed. Carmel McCarthy and John F. Healey, JSOT Supp 375 (New York: T. & T. Clark, 2004), 2–21.

4. Andrew Lear, "Ancient Pederasty: An Introduction," in *A Companion to Greek and Roman Sexualities*, ed. Thomas Hubbard (Chichester: Blackwell, 2014), 119.

5. Lear, "Ancient Pederasty," 117.

6. See Philo, *On the Contemplative Life* 59–61 and *On the Special Laws* 3:36–39; Josephus, *Jewish Antiquities* 1.200.

7. Lucretius, *On the Nature of the Universe* 4.4; Plato, *Laws* 636c; Musonius Rufus, *On Sexual Indulgence* (VII: Lutz). See also Karen Keen, "Sexuality, Critical Issues," in *Lexham Bible Dictionary*, ed. John D. Barry and Lazarus Wentz (Bellingham, WA: Logos Bible Software, 2014).

8. Across the ancient Near East, sexual norms were very similar to those of Israel (patricentric with tight control of women's sexuality). The portrait of

wildly sexually deviant nations is largely a slur, probably to denigrate the worship of other gods.

9. Traditionalists and progressives agree on many of the reasons why homoeroticism was condemned. Traditionalist Robert Gagnon and progressive James Brownson give essentially the same answer (although Gagnon emphasizes anatomical complementarity). Gagnon writes: "Rejection of same-sex intercourse on the grounds that it resulted in an infertile union was commonplace among Greeks and Romans. . . . Among post-biblical Jewish authors, Josephus and Philo also witness this view. . . . By putting themselves in the position of being 'mounted' by other men, the passive partners were regarded as willingly taking on not only a gender role contradictory to their anatomy but also the inferior nature and status of the woman. . . . In their descriptions of the sins of the men of Sodom, both Philo and Josephus describe a man's desire for sexual intercourse with other males as an insatiable overflow of lust beyond heterosexual intercourse" (*The Bible and Homosexual Practice: Texts and Hermeneutics* [Nashville: Abingdon, 2001], 164, 166, 169–70, 176–77). Brownson writes: "Almost all studies of homoeroticism in the ancient world recognize that the nearly universal pattern of same-sex erotic relationships in the ancient world (particularly among men) involved status differences between the active and passive partners. . . . For a man, to be penetrated is to be inherently degraded—that is, forced to act like a woman instead of a man. . . . We also find more specific references to same-sex eroticism as an expression of insatiable lust in Greco-Roman sources. . . . The early Jewish philosopher-theologian Philo, writing a bit earlier than Paul, makes a similar equation between same-sex eroticism and self-centered lust that refuses any boundaries. . . . In the ancient world generally, nature was understood to teach that sex was for the purpose of procreation. There is no reason to think that the references to nature in Romans 1 assume any other frame of reference" (*Bible, Gender, Sexuality: Reframing the Church's Debate on Same-Sex Relationships* [Grand Rapids: Eerdmans, 2013], 82, 154–55, 240).

10. Preston Sprinkle, a traditionalist scholar, acknowledges the strong procreation motif in the Old Testament but suggests procreation in marriage was minimized in first-century Judaism, including the New Testament (*Two Views on Homosexuality, the Bible, and the Church* [Grand Rapids: Zondervan, 2016], 219–22). For example, he points to Pseudo-Philo 50:1–5, a retelling of Hannah's story. Hannah says doing the will of God is more valuable than bearing children. Yet this story does not downplay the importance of procreation. In fact, it goes on to show that Hannah's prayer for a son is answered. The writer refutes a common belief that barrenness is a sign of sinfulness. This apology is also found in Wisdom of Solomon (3:13b–4:6). Sexual pleasure was affirmed alongside procreation, but without modern birth control the two could not be separated. In antiquity, having sex resulted in procreation. Both Paul and Jesus downplayed *marriage*. They did not envision a new paradigm of childless marriages. The new paradigm was *celibacy*. Paul counseled celibacy for people who wanted to avoid family entanglements.

11. Philo, *On the Life of Abraham* 135–37, trans. F. H. Colson, Loeb Classical Library, vol. VI (Cambridge: Harvard University Press, 1984), 71.

12. Josephus, *Against Apion* 2.199, trans. William Whiston, *The New Complete Works of Josephus* (Grand Rapids: Kregel, 1999).

13. Augustine, *On Marriage and Concupiscence* 20.35.

14. I will not be discussing the debate on whether Romans 1 refers to female same-sex relations. The evidence is ambiguous. For that discussion, see Bernadette Brooten, who argues for homoeroticism (*Love Between Women: Early Christian Responses to Female Homoeroticism* [Chicago: University of Chicago Press, 1996], 246–53), and James Brownson, who argues for heteroeroticism (*Bible, Gender, Sexuality*, 207–9). Since the crux of the debate is complementarity, the inclusion of women is assumed for traditionalists. This book engages the conversation with that in mind. However, it's important to realize that early on Romans 1 was not always understood and interpreted as referring to female same-sex relations. This underscores the importance of entering the world of the biblical authors rather than superimposing our modern assumptions on them.

Notes to Chapter 3

1. The six proof texts are Gen. 19, Lev. 18:22 and 20:13, Rom. 1:26–27, 1 Cor. 6:9–10, and 1 Tim. 1:9–10. Some proof text lists also include Deut. 23:17–18 and Jude 6–7. Other pertinent verses are Gen. 9:20–24, Judg. 19:22–25, Mark 7:17–23 (*porneia*; see also Matt. 15:10–20 and Acts 15:28–29), and Rev. 22:15. Note that the debate centers not on these verses (with the exception of Rom. 1 and, sometimes, the Levitical prohibitions) but on the Genesis narratives and the concept of complementarity.

2. Traditionalists acknowledge that aspects of gender are socially constructed. But they argue that scientific studies and basic observation demonstrate that men and women are not the same, if for no other reason than hormonal influences or the way the brain develops in utero. The existence of transgender people also indicates gender is not merely socially constructed or entirely flexible. Transgender people have a very strong sense of gender that seems to be hardwired in some way. However, traditionalists tend to see the transgender experience as psychological.

3. Robert Gagnon, *The Bible and Homosexual Practice: Texts and Hermeneutics* (Nashville: Abingdon, 2001), 289–91.

4. For a discussion of Genesis and Revelation as bookends for an overarching biblical portrait of marriage, see N. T. Wright, "What Is Marriage For?" *Plough Quarterly* 6 (2015): 38–43.

5. The Hebrew word *ezer* is often translated as "helper," giving the impression that the woman is a subordinate. But in the Old Testament *ezer* is used most

often of God intervening to deliver helpless humanity from distress (e.g., Exod. 18:4; Deut. 33:7; Ps. 33:20). A better translation is "strong ally."

6. Gagnon asserts that Adam and Eve were created from an androgynous being and that through marriage male and female are two halves reunited into a "single composite being" (Gagnon, *Bible and Homosexual Practice*, 61; Dan O. Via and Robert A. J. Gagnon, *Homosexuality and the Bible: Two Views* [Minneapolis: Fortress, 2003], 61). Setting aside the negative implications for unmarried people as incomplete, this view is not stated in Scripture but stems from Greek philosophy (see Aristophanes's speech in Plato's *Symposium*). When the apostle Paul reads Genesis, he interprets the first human being as Adam and fully male, not androgynous (1 Cor. 11:12; see also 1 Tim. 2:13).

7. The wording of "one flesh" and "flesh of my flesh" refers to kinship. See Gen. 29:14; Judg. 9:2; 2 Sam. 5:1; 19:12–13; 1 Chron. 11:1. See also James Brownson, *Bible, Gender, Sexuality: Reframing the Church's Debate on Same-Sex Relationships* (Grand Rapids: Eerdmans, 2013), 29–38.

8. The Qumran community seems to have known a tradition without "two"; the *Damascus Document* argues against polygyny but does not use "two" in Gen. 2:24 as evidence to make the case (David Instone-Brewer, *Divorce and Remarriage in the Bible: The Social and Literary Context* [Grand Rapids: Eerdmans, 2002], 61). The writer possibly knew a Masoretic Text tradition or another Hebrew tradition that also did not have "two."

9. Instone-Brewer, *Divorce and Remarriage*, 61, 137.

10. Israelite perspectives on marriage are not nearly as romantic as traditionalists portray. Polygyny (1 Sam. 25:39–43), levirate marriage (Gen. 38:6–10), and rapist-victim marriage (Deut. 22:28–29) were all acceptable. Men could also have sex with women other than their wives, including slaves and concubines. Sexuality did not become more restricted for Jewish men until perhaps the second century BCE as a result of the Greeks' promotion of marital monogamy in the ancient Near East. Only in the Greco-Roman period do we see extrabiblical Jewish writing that aggressively argues against polygyny.

One man/one woman marriage or sex is not the only form sanctioned in much of the Bible. The significance of this observation is that interpretation of the Bible involves decisions about what forms of marriage and sexual activity we accept (or not) from the biblical authors. Even traditionalists do not agree with everything the biblical authors propose about marriage. New Testament views are closer to traditionalists' arguments than the Old Testament, but even here we might disagree with certain conclusions, including Paul's instruction that a man could force a woman to remain unmarried if he decided that fate for her (1 Cor. 7:37). We might also disagree with Paul's reading of the Genesis narratives when he concludes that women are more easily deceived because Eve was deceived (1 Tim. 2:12–15).

11. For an in-depth discussion of the implications of Jesus's statement for same-sex relationships, see Robert Song, *Covenant and Calling: Towards a The-*

ology of Same-Sex Relationships (London: SCM, 2014). Song suggests the debate should be framed not as heterosexual vs. same-sex relationships, but rather as procreative vs. non-procreative relationships. He frames this within a theology of resurrection and eschatology.

12. Trent Horn, "Why the Church Cannot Marry the Impotent," *Catholic Answers*, August 7, 2014, https://www.catholic.com/magazine/online-edition/why-the-church-cannot-marry-the-impotent.

13. Brownson notes regarding gender norms: "Almost none of the texts cited by Gagnon to support his notion of 'anatomical complementarity' say anything about actual body parts. Instead, almost all of these passages speak negatively of how the passive partner in male-male sex is degraded, and either forced or deceived into abandoning his 'natural' manliness and acting like a woman instead. Jewish writers are particularly derisive of those passive partners in male-male sex who exhibit feminine appearance or behavior. In other words, what these early Jewish texts have in mind is not anatomical complementarity but the violation of socially normed gender roles" (*Bible, Gender, Sexuality*, 242). Some traditionalists recognize the problem of denying all same-sex relationships on the basis of anatomical complementarity alone and resort to arguments for gender and not strictly sexual complementarity. But the biblical authors understood gender in very rigid terms of active (male) and passive (female) roles. Their primary concern was to prevent men from assuming an inferior status, exemplified by a so-called feminine role in sex. This is why almost all (if not all) biblical texts that prohibit same-sex relations are directed exclusively to men. If the biblical authors had in mind mutual complementarity of masculine and feminine, we would expect them to give equal attention to women.

14. Brownson, *Bible, Gender, Sexuality*, 231–32.

15. William Loader, "Homosexuality and the Bible," in *Two Views on Homosexuality, the Bible, and the Church*, ed. Preston Sprinkle (Grand Rapids: Zondervan, 2016), 29.

16. Brownson states that, for the gay person, "to embrace the 'natural' union of male and female in marriage often leads to profound dislocation." *Bible, Gender, Sexuality*, 232.

17. Deut. 4:16–18 warns against idolatry using similar vocabulary as Rom. 1:23 (e.g., image, likeness, bird, reptile, male and female; see Septuagint). Traditionalists sometimes acknowledge these similarities but argue that the Deuteronomic writer had Genesis in mind. Notably, Gen. 1:26–27, which traditionalists use to compare with vocabulary in Rom. 1, says nothing about idolatry—the primary concern of Deut. 4 and Rom. 1. The literary and theological contexts are different and cannot be artificially conflated to fit a Genesis fall argument. Other verses in the Bible that use the same vocabulary as Rom. 1:23 include Acts 10:12 and 11:6, which describe Peter's vision of unclean animals (e.g., bird, reptile, four-footed animal).

18. For example, see Ben Witherington III, *Paul's Letter to the Romans: A*

Socio-Rhetorical Commentary (Grand Rapids: Eerdmans, 2004); Douglas Campbell, *The Deliverance of God: An Apocalyptic Rereading of Justification in Paul* (Grand Rapids: Eerdmans, 2009).

19. Anders Nygren, *Commentary on Romans*, trans. C. C. Rasmussen (London: SCM, 1952), 112–16.

20. Historically, the church perceived those with same-sex attraction as spiritually depraved. Martin Luther, for example, believed the devil caused the desires after a person rejected God. Today many traditionalists realize that people are not attracted to the same sex because of spiritual depravity; thus, new arguments have been proposed for interpreting Rom. 1, including claims that it refers to Christians who struggle with a fallen nature. Traditionalists know that if Paul *does* view same-sex attraction as stemming from willful spiritual corruption, their case is significantly challenged. In Rom. 1 Paul denounces not merely same-sex acts but also same-sex desire, which he understands as rooted in rejection of God.

21. For further critique on this, see Karen Kilby's discussion of Balthasar in chap. 6 of her book *Balthasar: A (Very) Critical Introduction* (Grand Rapids: Eerdmans, 2012), as well as the suggested articles in the Further Reading list at the end of this chapter. These address the problem of superimposing gender onto the Godhead. I am also grateful to friend and theologian Kirsten Guidero for sharing insights from her paper "Women and the Christ Form: Refining Balthasar on Gender" (Christians for Biblical Equality Annual Meeting, Pittsburgh, PA, July 2013).

22. James Brownson, "Response to a Review: How to Interpret Ephesians 5," personal blog, July 11, 2013, https://jimbrownson.wordpress.com/2013/06/11/response-to-a-review-how-to-interpret-ephesians-5/.

23. This also clarifies a common misinterpretation of Eph. 5 that parallels male headship with submission. The literary parallel is actually head and body. The husband and wife are, figuratively, one united person. For an excellent discussion of this, see Sarah Sumner, *Men and Women in the Church: Building Consensus on Christian Leadership* (Downers Grove, IL: InterVarsity Press, 2003).

Notes to Chapter 4

1. "Morocco Amends Controversial Rape Law," *BBC News*, January 23, 2014, http://www.bbc.com/news/world-africa-25855025.

2. The law collections are not to be confused with other legal texts such as court records or transactional documents that specify an actual case with names, location, and details of a particular situation. A separate archeological collection of legal documents pertains to actual daily legal affairs. Significant debate exists regarding the relationship between the law collections and the transactional and court records because these other records do not directly

refer to the law collections (Martha T. Roth, *Law Collections from Mesopotamia and Asia Minor*, ed. Piotr Michalowski [Atlanta: Scholars Press, 1997], 16). For example, court records do not say, "We are rendering this judgment in accordance with law 52 of the Hammurabi collection." Various theories have been proposed about how much the law collections were used in daily legal affairs. Many of the law collections have been found in scribal schools, and the casuistry style of the texts is in the vein of the Mesopotamian genre of scientific inquiry (Raymond Westbrook, ed., *A History of Ancient Near Eastern Law*, 2 vols. [Boston: Brill, 2003], 17–18). Thus, some scholars believe the collections were used for educational purposes—for teaching and dialoguing about legal matters. Others propose the law collections were royal propaganda to validate the authority of the king. Still others think they were a form of common law that was enforced. Scholars do agree that there is a distinction between the law collections and the daily legal records, but there is no clear consensus on what that distinction means.

3. All translations of ancient Near Eastern law collections (aside from the biblical text) are from Roth, *Law Collections*.

4. The NIV reads "gives birth prematurely," but states in a footnote "or has a miscarriage." Scholars debate which is the case. But either way, the woman experiences an act of violence that affects her unborn child.

5. For a good overview of these various categories of laws within ancient Near Eastern collections, see Samuel A. Jackson, *A Comparison of Ancient Near Eastern Law Collections Prior to the First Millennium BC* (Piscataway, NJ: Gorgias Press, 2008); Raymond Westbrook, ed., *A History of Ancient Near Eastern Law*, 2 vols. (Leiden: Brill, 2003).

6. Bill T. Arnold and Bryan E. Beyer, *Readings from the Ancient Near East: Primary Sources for Old Testament Study* (Grand Rapids: Baker Academic, 2002), 112.

7. For a brief discussion of motive clauses in Old Testament laws, see Waldemar Janzen, *Old Testament Ethics: A Paradigmatic Approach* (Louisville: Westminster John Knox, 1994), 60–62, 81n12.

8. Gen. 18:19 (Abraham); 1 Chron. 18:14 (King David); 1 Kings 10:9 (Solomon); Jer. 33:15 (Messiah); Ps. 89:14 (God).

9. F. Brown, S. Driver, and C. Briggs, *The Brown-Driver-Briggs Hebrew and English Lexicon* (Peabody, MA: Hendrickson, 2003); H. W. F. Gesenius, *Gesenius' Hebrew-Chaldee Lexicon to the Old Testament*, 7th ed., trans. Samuel Prideaux Tregelles (Grand Rapids: Baker, 1990).

10. Many English translations render *shalom* as "peace," but that does not capture the full essence of the term, which conveys wholeness, health, and welfare.

11. Brown, Driver, and Briggs, *Lexicon*; Gesenius, *Lexicon*.

Notes to Chapter 5

1. To understand a conservative interpretive explanation for why some directives—like the wearing of head coverings—can be dismissed but not others, see Benjamin L. Merkle, "Should Women Wear Head Coverings?," Gospel Coalition, August 26, 2015, https://www.thegospelcoalition.org/article/should-women-wear-head-coverings.

2. I realize progressives might disagree with the prohibition being a creation ordinance. However, this chapter is geared toward addressing the concerns and objections of traditionalists.

3. Richard Hays, *Moral Vision of the New Testament: Community, Cross, and New Creation: A Contemporary Introduction to New Testament Ethics* (New York: HarperOne, 1996), 209. Hays names four modes of appealing to Scripture: rules, principles, paradigms, and symbolic worlds. His book offers one helpful example (among others) of how to think about appropriating ethics from the Bible.

4. Another common progressive argument is liberation for the oppressed. However, that argument is not as strong. While the Bible clearly speaks to liberation, such an argument assumes the innocence of those who are oppressed, an assumption not held by traditionalists. To a traditionalist's ears, the liberation argument sounds like: "We need to liberate people into hedonism!"

5. This is evident in a debate between New Testament scholar Preston Sprinkle and Christian philosopher Jeff Cook. Cook affirms same-sex relationships based on virtue ethics, but Sprinkle doesn't believe that virtue replaces the importance of rules. See their entire debate, titled "Preston Sprinkle and Jeff Cook: A Debate on Homosexuality," on Sprinkle's personal blog (2015), https://www.prestonsprinkle.com/blogs/theologyintheraw/2015/06/preston-sprinkle-and-jeff-cook-a-debate-about-homosexuality.

6. Traditionalists include "violation of the created order" as a definition of sin. But given the New Testament's emphasis on violating the fruit of the Spirit as the criterion for sin, it's not clear that this assumption is warranted.

7. The italicized text is in the Masoretic Text version of Isa. 2:9–11 but not the Great Isaiah Scroll: "So people will be brought low and everyone humbled—*do not forgive them. Go into the rocks, hide in the ground from the fearful presence of the* LORD *and the splendor of his majesty!* The eyes of the arrogant will be humbled and human pride brought low; the LORD alone will be exalted in that day." One can see how the italicized text interrupts the original flow.

8. Joseph Blenkinsopp, *A History of Prophecy in Israel*, rev. ed. (Louisville: Westminster John Knox, 1996), 130–35.

9. To learn more about the differences and to read the two versions of Jeremiah for yourself, see my blog post, "The Quest for the Original Bible," March 9, 2018, https://karenkeen.com/2018/03/09/the-quest-for-the-original-bible/.

10. Other revisions are unrelated to ethics. For example, the author

of Chronicles drastically changes the profile of King Manasseh. In 2 Kings, Manasseh is the most wicked ruler of Judah and is responsible for the destruction and exile of God's people (21:1–18). In 2 Chronicles he is portrayed as humble and repentant (33:1–20). For more on legal revisions, see Bernard M. Levinson's *Legal Revision and Religious Renewal in Ancient Israel* (Cambridge: Cambridge University Press, 2008) and *Deuteronomy and the Hermeneutics of Legal Innovation* (New York: Oxford University Press, 1997).

11. The NIV uses the word "servant" rather than "slave." But this is a poor rendering. In English, "servant" is usually understood to mean a hired or volunteer worker. That is not what the Hebrew word *ebed* means here. In this context, it refers to a human being bought and sold as property. The word "slave" is the correct translation.

12. The NIV translates the sentence "sells themselves to you," but it can also be translated as "is sold to you." Most translations, including ESV, NASB, and KJV, all go with the latter rendering. But, if the NIV is correct, the author of Deuteronomy appears to be signaling opposition to slavery by changing the original rendering in Exodus from "If you buy" to the idea that slaves should be owned only if they sell themselves. This shifts the focus from the owner's business interests to the slave's interests. (A slave might sell himself or herself to escape poverty.)

13. For those who might be concerned about the contradiction in the biblical slavery laws (women not allowed to go free versus women allowed to go free), see R. W. L. Moberly's discussion on the phenomenon of disparity in Scripture in *Old Testament Theology: Reading the Hebrew Bible as Christian Scripture* (Grand Rapids: Baker Academic, 2013), 111–16.

14. The passage could be interpreted as saying that only male slaves receive the provisions upon going out. In a patricentric culture, a woman would have subsisted on the resources of male relatives. However, the statement "Do the same for your female slave" could be interpreted as including female slaves in the requirement to give provisions.

15. In the Levitical law, owning a Hebrew slave is outlawed; however, owning foreign slaves is still approved (Lev. 25:39–46).

16. One might ask why, if the law given at Mount Sinai was directly from God, God did not give the instructions clearly in the first place. That is a great question that helps us to begin looking at how we define the nature and function of Scripture as revelation. Paul acknowledged that prophecy is only "in part" and that we can know only "in part," for "we see only a reflection as in a mirror" (1 Cor. 13:9–12). Even Scripture is an example of that.

17. Jesus recognizes cultural distance from his own scriptural tradition. He refers to Deut. 24:1–4 not as God's law but as Moses's law. However, the writer of Deuteronomy saw these laws as inspired by God: "These are the decrees and laws you must be careful to follow in the land that the LORD, the God of your ancestors, has given you to possess—as long as you live in the land" (12:1; see

Deut. 11 for context). This statement refers to the laws listed in Deut. 12–26, commonly known as the Deuteronomic law collection. For more on understanding Old Testament law and why Jesus might have felt comfortable speaking of Scripture in this way, see Chapter 4.

18. Paul's writing is earlier than Mark, but he is clearly citing the tradition passed down to him that also appears in Mark. Traditionalist Richard Hays discusses this interpretive movement on divorce in *Moral Vision*, 353–61.

19. According to rabbinic commentary, the school of Hillel, which was prominent in the first century CE, interpreted Deut. 24:1 to mean a man could divorce his wife even for burning his food (Mishnah Gittin 9:10).

20. Notice how in Isa. 58 Sabbath observance is put in the same category as practicing justice, rather than merely observing ceremonial law. Indeed, according to the Mosaic law, honoring the Sabbath is a matter of justice because it required allowing slaves, laborers, and animals to have their rest too.

21. In addition to the points made in this chapter, also consider these biblical nuances to ethics:

1. *Discernment of context.* Proverbs 26:4–5 provides a good example of how to think about Scripture and ethics. One proverb says we should answer the fool. The other says we should not. These back-to-back maxims teach that we need to discern when and how to apply certain principles depending on the situation we are in. Sometimes it is good to answer the fool. Sometimes it is not.

2. *Discernment of conflicting ethical instructions.* What do we do when Scripture gives conflicting directives? For example, the biblical authors condemned same-sex relations, but Paul also directs those who are unable to remain celibate to marry and those who are married to not deprive each other (1 Cor. 7:5, 9, 36). A heterosexual person, even if temporarily single, has options for pursuing marriage and following this advice. How do gay people apply these ethical instructions? We have to use discernment, which involves some level of subjectivity.

3. *Discernment of the heart's intentions.* Paul said that even though eating meat sacrificed to idols is not sin, if you *think* it is sin and eat it anyway, you are guilty (Rom. 14:21–23). In this case, no law is violated, but the person is still guilty. The issue is the intentions of one's heart. So also, if you do break a command *but don't realize it*, God is not as concerned (Luke 12:47–48; see also 23:34). Jesus said to the religious leaders, "If you were blind, you would not be guilty of sin; but now that you claim you can see, your guilt remains" (John 9:41). What constitutes sin depends, in part, on our conscience and our heart's intentions. How might this affect how a traditionalist relates to someone who genuinely believes a same-sex partnership is not sin?

Notes to Chapter 6

1. Focus on the Family, "Abortion and the 'Health of the Mother,'" Family Q&A, 2010, https://www.focusonthefamily.com/family-q-and-a/pro-life/abortion-and-health-of-the-mother.

2. Paul R. Gilchrist, ed., "Report of the Ad-Interim Committee on Divorce and Remarriage to the Twentieth General Assembly," in *PCA Digest*, 3 vols. (1993), 2:229, http://www.pcahistory.org/pca/divorce-remarriage.pdf.

3. William Perkins, *Christian Oeconomie: Or, Household-Government, A Short Survey of the Right Manner of Erecting and Ordering a Family According to the Scriptures*, in *The Workes of that Famous and Worthy Minister of Christ in the Universitie of Cambridge*, 3 vols. (London: John Haviland, 1631), 3:688.

4. Gilchrist, "Report," 228, 252, 293.

5. For Ryan's story, see justbecausehebreathes.com; Rob and Linda's testimony at the Exodus Conference ("Just Because He Breathes," June, 20, 2013, https://youtu.be/P8ntauVWRUY); and their GCN talk ("Just Because He Breathes," April 23, 2015, https://youtu.be/Jk_-9Jlx1Bs).

6. Traditionalist authors Kevin DeYoung and Preston Sprinkle downplay the reality of lifelong celibacy, suggesting sexual orientation change or heterosexual marriage before giving attention to celibacy. Neither seriously considers that lifelong celibacy might not be possible for everyone. Sprinkle carelessly quotes an anonymous friend who reports a 50 percent change rate for his clients. No name or citation is given to verify or test this claim. And such a percentage is quite out of sync with actual studies. Kevin DeYoung, *What Does the Bible Really Teach about Homosexuality?* (Wheaton, IL: Crossway, 2015), 109–15; Preston Sprinkle, *People to Be Loved: Why Homosexuality Is Not Just an Issue* (Grand Rapids: Zondervan, 2015), 157–75.

7. Mixed-orientation marriages exist and can be successful for some, but they do have higher rates of divorce. Most gay people do not have enough sexual flexibility to function heterosexually. Sex is not everything to a marriage, but it is a crucial aspect. Regardless of the causes of same-sex attraction, sexual orientation has been shown to be fairly fixed for most gay and lesbian people. Sexual fluidity, which is different than sexual orientation change, occurs more often among women than men. But not all women with same-sex attraction experience fluidity or flexibility. For more on causes of attraction to the same sex, see this excellent summary of the research: J. Michael Bailey et al., "Sexual Orientation, Controversy, and Science," *Psychological Science in the Public Interest* 17 (2016): 45–101.

8. Stanton L. Jones and Mark A. Yarhouse, *Homosexuality: The Use of Scientific Research in the Church's Moral Debate* (Downers Grove, IL: InterVarsity Press, 2000), 121. They also point out that previous studies that inflated rates of success were problematic: "Most of the published empirical studies on change were conducted during the 1950s, 1960s and 1970s. . . . The early research

on change was often of poor methodological quality by today's standards. . . . Measures of change in the older research, for example, were often based on the judgments of the persons serving as therapists, and often these ratings used categories (such as Very Improved and Somewhat Improved) that fail to provide detailed information about change. When the patients themselves were queried, their self-reports were again quite simplistic. . . . Use of therapists' ratings is par-ticular[ly] problematic by today's standards, based on concern that the therapists have a vested interest in reporting their own success. Rigorous examination of indices of sexual orientation were rarely if ever used" (121).

9. Stanton L. Jones and Mark A. Yarhouse, "'Ex-Gays?' An Extended Lon-gitudinal Study of Attempted Religiously Mediated Change in Sexual Orienta-tion," *Journal of Sex and Marital Therapy* 37 (2011): 404–27. This article provides a summary. See also the book by the same title.

10. J. P. Dehlin et al., "Sexual Orientation Change Efforts among Current or Former LDS Church Members," *Journal of Counseling Psychology* 62 (2015): 95–105. See also his presentation at Calvin College: "Sexual Orientation, Change, & Healing. Part 1: Research," https://livestream.com/calvin-college/Sexuality Series/videos/150168177.

11. Warren Throckmorton, "New SAMHSA Report Calls for End to Change Therapy for LGBT Youth," personal blog, October 15, 2015, http://www.wthrock morton.com/2015/10/15/new-samhsa-report-calls-for-end-to-change-therapy -for-lgbt-youth/.

12. Some confusion in the discussion occurs because those who experience sexual fluidity or flexibility are lumped together with those who do not. The fact that someone used to be in a same-sex relationship but now is married to the opposite sex does not necessarily indicate a change in sexual orientation. For example, some ex-gays who proclaimed healing were bisexual or experienced sexual fluidity. Joe Dallas, a prominent spokesperson for the ex-gay movement, acknowledges a history of relationships with both women and men. Rosaria Butterfield, who has never been part of the ex-gay movement but is nevertheless touted as ex-gay by many conservatives, had heterosexual relationships until her late twenties before she began dating women. That does not mean shifts in sexual orientation don't occur for a small percentage, but it's false and unethical to hold up singular cases as evidence that anyone can become heterosexual.

13. P. Bearman and H. Brückner, "After the Promise: The STD Conse-quences of Adolescent Virginity Pledges," *Journal of Adolescent Health* 36 (2005): 271–78. Some research indicates that pledgers with high religiosity show greater levels of success than pledgers who do not have a high level of religious commit-ment. However, the Grey Matter study (see note 16 below) was conservative in its definition of evangelical (i.e., in the way it tested for level of religious com-mitment). Thus, even a conservative estimate provides a high rate of 44 percent of evangelicals having had nonmarital sex by age twenty-nine.

14. Janet Elise Rosenbaum, "Patient Teenagers? A Comparison of the Sex-

ual Behavior of Virginity Pledgers and Non-Matched Pledgers," *Pediatrics* 123 (2009): 110–20.

15. Gary Thomas, "Marry Sooner Rather than Later," *Boundless*, March 13, 2009, http://www.boundless.org/relationships/2009/marry-sooner-rather -than-later.

16. The 80 percent figure is from a December 2009 study conducted by the National Campaign to Prevent Teen and Unplanned Pregnancy. For more, see Tyler Charles, "(Almost) Everyone Is Doing It," *Relevant* 53 (2011). The 44 percent figure is from a 2012 Grey Matter Research and Consulting study in col- laboration with the National Association of Evangelicals titled "Sex and Unex- pected Pregnancies: What Evangelical Millennials Think and Practice" (https:// www.nae.net/sex-and-unexpected-pregnancies/). Of note, the Grey Matter study did not define "sexually active." If participants interpreted the question as referring to sexual intercourse, that would exclude a lot of other types of sexual involvement. For example, oral sex might not be defined as sex, yet such activity clearly indicates the person is not celibate. Further study is needed to confirm these results.

17. A. W. Richard Sipe, *Celibacy in Crisis: A Secret World Revisited* (New York: Brunner-Routledge, 2003).

18. Men could lose their inheritance, and women had to remarry within two years if divorced or widowed. However, families with at least three children were rewarded. The rare exceptions to marriage in Roman society were Vestal Virgins and eunuchs. The relevant Roman laws are *Lex Iulia de maritandis ordinibus* and *Lex Papia Poppaea*. For more on this, see Raymond F. Collins, *Accompanied by a Believing Wife: Ministry and Celibacy in the Earliest Christian Communities* (Collegeville, MN: Liturgical Press, 2013), 66–68.

19. The following discussion on purity draws from William Loader, *Making Sense of Sex: Attitudes towards Sexuality in Early Jewish and Christian Litera- ture* (Grand Rapids: Eerdmans, 2013), 91–104, as well as Collins, *Believing Wife*.

20. Philo considered Moses to be in a permanent state of purity to con- verse with God (*On the Life of Moses* 2.68–69).

21. For Loader's discussion on this, specifically, see *Making Sense*, 91–92, 100.

22. April D. DeConick, *The Thirteenth Apostle: What the Gospel of Judas Really Says*, rev. ed. (London: Continuum, 2009), 17–19.

23. The reason for associating Adam and Eve's disobedience with sexual desire is that they are not depicted as having sex until after their rebellion (Gen. 4:1). Obviously, this theology conflicts with the goodness of sex and procreation in Genesis.

24. Ambrose, *Concerning Virginity* 1.5.23, 35, in *Nicene and Post-Nicene Fathers*, Second Series, vol. 10, ed. Philip Schaff and Henry Wace, trans. H. de Romestin, E. de Romestin, and H. T. F. Duckworth (Buffalo, NY: Christian Lit- erature, 1896); revised and edited for New Advent by Kevin Knight, http://www. newadvent.org/fathers/34071.htm.

25. Augustine, *On Genesis Literally Interpreted* 5.2.7–12, trans. John Hammond Taylor (New York: Newman Press, 1982), 77.

26. Annemarie Kidder, *Women, Celibacy, and the Church* (New York: Crossroad, 2003), 171–73.

27. Martin Luther, "Commentary on 1 Corinthians 7," in *Commentaries on 1 Corinthians 7, 1 Corinthians 15, Lectures on 1 Timothy*, Luther's Works 28, ed. Edward Sittler (St. Louis: Concordia, 1973), 25–31.

28. The lack of deliberative process is also affecting how young people view Scripture and sexual ethics. Unlike older generations who were more likely to believe ghost stories about gay people, young people have gay friends. They know the ghost stories aren't true. They can intuit that mandatory lifelong celibacy for their friends is problematic. Thus, young people increasingly assume the church must be prescribing archaic sexual ethics in general, leading to greater acceptance of nonmarital sex. Ironically, traditionalists' unwillingness to extend marital covenant to gay and lesbian people has contributed to the deconstruction of covenant.

Contrary to many traditionalists' concerns, marriage of same-sex couples will not erode the institution of marriage. Covenant fidelity has suffered since the advent of contraception and no-fault divorce, which made sex without covenant easier. This does not mean all forms of contraception or divorce are immoral. Rather, the church would do well to help restore an admiration of and value for covenant. This can be stimulated, in part, by allowing gay and lesbian people to participate in covenant fidelity.

29. Focus on the Family, "Focus on the Family's Position on Marriage and Divorce," Family Q&A (2010), https://www.focusonthefamily.com/family-q-and-a/relationships-and-marriage/focus-on-the-familys-position-on-marriage-and-divorce.

30. Gilchrist, "Report," 252. The PCA rightly acknowledges that in antiquity a Jewish writ of divorce automatically freed a person to remarry. Jesus and Paul, both Jews, understood divorce and remarriage in this way. "Christ allowed for a bill of divorce to be given in the case of *porneia*. The essential text of such a bill of divorce recorded in the Mishnah is, 'Lo, thou art free to marry any man.' The Mishnah goes on to record the wording of Rabbi Judah: 'Let this be from me thy writ of divorce and letter of dismissal and deed of liberation, that thou mayest marry whatsoever man thou wilt.' Whether or not this was the divorce bill text envisioned by Deuteronomy 24:1 is not germane. Christ was commenting on current custom and application of that law. In other words, in Jesus's day, divorce carried with it the right to remarriage, and that would have been understood in their discussions" ("Report," 205).

31. Gilchrist, "Report," 230.

32. Gilchrist, "Report," 229–30.

Notes to Chapter 7

1. Rosaria Champagne Butterfield, *Openness Unhindered: Further Thoughts of an Unlikely Convert on Sexual Identity and Union with Christ* (Pittsburgh: Crown & Covenant, 2015), 94–98.

2. Butterfield, *Openness Unhindered*, 123. Butterfield says she does not believe temptation is sin. Yet it's not clear how she distinguishes between temptation and unintentional sexual desire. She also deems unintentional heterosexual attraction toward a non-spouse sinful. Her perspective may be based, in part, on views that concupiscence itself is sin. Not all Christian traditions take that view (see the "Decree Concerning Original Sin" at the fifth session of the Council of Trent). The implication is that puberty leads to a sinful state since the very nature of puberty is the development of sexual attraction that is not locked or unlocked on the basis of marital status. Butterfield's view fails to distinguish basic human biological realities from lust.

3. Butterfield, *Openness Unhindered*, 125. Likely, if she acknowledges innate origin, she attributes it to the fallen state. Either way, she considers it moral fallenness and not natural fallenness.

4. Wesley Hill, "Response to William Loader" and "Christ, Scripture, and Spiritual Friendship," in *Two Views on Homosexuality, the Bible, and the Church*, ed. Preston Sprinkle (Grand Rapids: Zondervan, 2016), 55–60, 134–37.

5. Hill, "Response to William Loader," 57.

6. Dennis R. Venema, "Genesis and the Genome: Genomics Evidence for Human-Ape Common Ancestry and Ancestral Hominid Population Sizes," *Perspectives on Science and Christian Faith* 62 (2010): 166–78.

7. For further discussion on the Bible and evolution, see John H. Walton, *The Lost World of Genesis One: Ancient Cosmology and the Origins Debate* (Downers Grove, IL: InterVarsity Press, 2009); Peter Enns, *The Evolution of Adam: What the Bible Does and Doesn't Say about Human Origins* (Grand Rapids: Brazos, 2012); Kyle Greenwood, *Scripture and Cosmology: Reading the Bible Between the Ancient World and Modern Science* (Downers Grove, IL: InterVarsity Press, 2015); Scot McKnight and Dennis R. Venema, *Adam and the Genome: Reading Scripture after Genetic Science* (Grand Rapids: Brazos, 2017). "William Stone," an evangelical paleontologist who uses a pseudonym to avoid rejection by academic colleagues, believes in a historical Adam and denies human evolution from primates. Yet he concedes the evidence raises questions, including DNA from extinct *Homo* species. Attempting to resolve this, he proposes we locate Adam 1.8 million years ago with *Homo erectus/ergaster*. But he admits that 1.8 million years ago does not match the genealogies in the Bible that date the first man to about six thousand years ago. Even if we place Adam with the first *Homo sapiens*, we are talking about at least two hundred thousand years ago. See Stone's discussion in "Adam and Modern Science," in *Adam, the Fall, and Original Sin: Theological, Biblical,*

and Scientific Perspectives, ed. Hans Madueme and Michael Reeves (Grand Rapids: Baker Academic, 2014), 78.

8. An accessible explanation is offered by scientist Dennis R. Venema in an article at the BioLogos website titled "Mitochondrial Eve, Y-Chromosome Adam, and Reasons to Believe," October 28, 2011, http://biologos.org/blogs/dennis -venema-letters-to-the-duchess/mitochondrial-eve-y-chromosome-adam-and -reasons-to-believe.

9. Significantly, the author of Gen. 3 indicates that evil and mortality existed prior to Adam and Eve's disobedience. In the parabolic garden scene, the serpent is present with Adam and Eve before they sin. The conniving reptile seduces and deceives. Jewish tradition found in Wisdom of Solomon blames the serpent for starting the downfall (2:24). The Genesis account also portrays human mortality as inherent to original creation and not the result of sin. Otherwise the tree of life, which is *external* to the first human beings, makes little sense. Only if they ate from the tree of life would they become immortal (Gen. 3:22–23). The couple is protected from immortalizing their fallen state by expulsion from the garden. In other words, they don't lose an original immortality; they lose the opportunity to obtain it.

10. P. Kervella, "ALMA Observations of the Nearby AGB Star L2 Puppis: I. Mass of the Central Star and Detection of a Candidate Planet," *Astronomy and Astrophysics* 596 (2016), https://www.aanda.org/articles/aa/abs/2016/12/ aa29877-16/aa29877-16.html; Nola Taylor Redd, "Red Giant Stars: Facts, Definition, and the Future of the Sun," Space.com, March 27, 2018, https://www.space .com/22471-red-giant-stars.html.

11. The above discussion raises some questions. If humanity was born into an environment that already included evil and death, that suggests God may have created evil and death, challenging God's goodness. However, the existence of continued evil and suffering alongside an all-powerful God remains a mystery regardless and is not fully resolved by an Adamic origin of sin. For a start on this conversation, see Neil Messer, "Natural Evil after Darwin," in *Theology after Darwin*, ed. Michael S. Northcott and R. J. Berry (Colorado Springs: Paternoster, 2009), 139–54.

12. John Walton, "Historical Adam," in *Four Views on the Historical Adam*, ed. Matthew Barrett and Ardel B. Caneday (Grand Rapids: Zondervan, 2013), 107.

13. Hans Madueme, "'The Most Vulnerable Part of the Whole Christian Account': Original Sin and Modern Science," in *Adam, the Fall, and Original Sin*, ed. Madueme and Reeves, 246–47.

14. For the following summary I draw from an excellent overview of the research by Bailey et al., in addition to the other sources I cite. See J. Michael Bailey et al., "Sexual Orientation, Controversy, and Science," *Psychological Science in the Public Interest* 17 (2016): 45–101.

15. A 2011 Williams Institute study by Gary Gates titled "How Many Peo-

ple Are Lesbian, Gay, Bisexual, and Transgender?" indicates that 1.7 percent identify as gay or lesbian and 1.8 percent as bisexual—that is, 3.5 percent of the population. However, the same report found that 8.2 percent of Americans had experienced same-sex activity and 11 percent had experienced some attraction to the same sex. One study of Facebook data found that in states where there is less acceptance, people underreport their same-sex attractions. This study estimates that about 5 percent of men are gay (Seth Stephens-Davidowitz, "Everybody Lies: How Google Search Reveals Our Darkest Secrets," *The Guardian*, July 9, 2017, https://www.theguardian.com/technology/2017/jul/09/everybody -lies-how-google-reveals-darkest-secrets-seth-stephens-davidowitz). Overall, most studies tend to fall in the range of 3–5 percent if that includes those who are bisexual. For comparison, Jews comprise about 2.2 percent of the US population.

16. Mark Yarhouse et al., "Experiences of Students and Alumni Navigating Sexual Identity in Faith-Based Higher Education: A Qualitative Study," *Growth Journal* 14 (2015): 16–27.

17. M. K. McClintock and G. Herdt, "Rethinking Puberty: The Development of Sexual Attraction," *Current Directions in Psychological Science* 5 (1996): 178–83; G. Herdt and M. K. McClintock, "The Magical Age of 10," *Archives of Sexual Behavior* 29 (2000): 587–606.

18. Bailey et al., "Sexual Orientation," 57–58.

19. Historically, treatments that gay people have undergone or been violently subjected to have included lobotomy, electroshock therapy, "corrective rape" (mostly in non-Western countries), psychoanalysis, heterosexual marriage (with hope of it changing attractions), exorcism, castration, hormone therapy, use of heterosexual pornography, and more. None of these has succeeded in changing most gay people's sexual orientation. A very small minority report a shift to bisexuality with therapy or a support group. (See the discussion in Chapter 6.)

20. A small group of conservatives continue to promote the view of dysfunctional parent-child relationships without sufficient evidence. NARTH (rebranded as Alliance for Therapeutic Choice and Scientific Integrity) is the main proponent of this view. For a critique of reparative theory, see a collection of blog articles on the topic at Dr. Warren Throckmorton's site (Throckmorton is an evangelical psychologist): "Reparative Therapy Information," http://www .wthrockmorton.com/reparative-therapy-information/.

21. H. Wilson and C. Widom, "Does Physical Abuse, Sexual Abuse, or Neglect in Childhood Increase the Likelihood of Same-Sex Sexual Relationships and Cohabitation? A Prospective 30-year Follow-up," *Archives of Sexual Behavior* 39 (2010): 63–74.

22. David W. Purcell, Jocelyn D. Patterson, and Pilgrim S. Spikes Jr., "Childhood Sexual Abuse Experienced by Gay and Bisexual Men: Understanding the Disparities and Interventions," in *Unequal Opportunity: Health Disparities*

Affecting Gay and Bisexual Men in the United States, ed. Richard Wolitski, Ron Stall, and Ronald O. Valdiserri (New York: Oxford University Press, 2008), 74.

23. Lisa Diamond, *Sexual Fluidity: Understanding Women's Love and Desire* (Cambridge, MA: Harvard University Press, 2009).

24. Kenneth S. Kendler et al., "Sexual Orientation in a U.S. National Sample of Twin and Nontwin Sibling Pairs," *American Journal of Psychiatry* 157 (2000): 1843–46; A. R. Sanders et al., "Genome-wide Scan Demonstrates Significant Linkage for Male Sexual Orientation," *Psychological Medicine* 45 (2015): 1379–88.

25. See W. R. Rice et al., "Homosexuality as a Consequence of Epigenetically Canalized Sexual Development," *Quarterly Review of Biology* 87 (2012): 343–68.

26. Bailey et al., "Sexual Orientation," 79-80; D. P. VanderLaan and P. L. Vasey, "Male Sexual Orientation in Independent Samoa: Evidence for Fraternal Birth Order and Maternal Fecundity Effects," *Archives of Sexual Behavior* 40 (2011): 495–503; R. Blanchard, "Fraternal Birth Order, Family Size, and Male Homosexuality: Meta-Analysis of Studies Spanning 25 Years," *Archives of Sexual Behavior* (2017), https://www.ncbi.nlm.nih.gov/pubmed/28608293.

27. Anthony F. Bogaert et al., "Male Homosexuality and Maternal Immune Responsivity to the Y-linked Protein NLGN4Y," *Proceedings of the National Academy of Sciences of the United States of America* 115 (2018): 302–6.

28. For an overview, see Arthur P. Arnold, "The Organizational-Activational Hypothesis as the Foundation for a Unified Theory of Sexual Differentiation of All Mammalian Tissues," *Hormones and Behavior* 55 (2009): 570–78.

29. V. L. Pasterski et al., "Prenatal Hormones versus Postnatal Socialization by Parents as Determinants of Male-Typical Toy Play in Girls with Congenital Adrenal Hyperplasia," *Child Development* 76 (2005): 264–78. The comparable situation for XY babies is androgen deficiency syndrome (AIS). Babies affected by this intersex condition are typically raised as girls and attracted to males. But what happens if a male fetus responds normally to androgens and then is raised as a girl from infancy? A study of seven boys who lost their penises post-birth and were raised as girls suggests that prenatal androgens determined their sexual orientation. Despite being socialized as girls, they did not develop an attraction to boys. Significantly, the difference between them and those with AIS is response to prenatal androgens. For this discussion, see Bailey et al., "Sexual Orientation," 72–74.

30. Antonio Guillamon, Carme Junque, and Esther Gomez-Gil, "A Review of the Status of Brain Structure Research in Transsexualism," *Archives of Sexual Behavior* 45 (2016): 1615–48.

31. Jorge Ponseti et al., "Homosexual Women Have Less Grey Matter in Perirhinal Cortex than Heterosexual Women," *PLoS ONE* 2 (2007): e762, https://doi.org/10.1371/journal.pone.0000762.

32. Charles E. Roselli, Radhika Reddy, and Katherine Kaufman, "The Development of Male-Oriented Behavior in Rams," *Frontiers in Neuroendocrinology* 32 (2011): 164–69.

33. For example, see Kathryn Burtinshaw and Dr. John Burt, *Lunatics, Imbeciles and Idiots: A History of Insanity in Nineteenth-Century Britain & Ireland* (Barnsley: Pen and Sword, 2017).

34. See Adrienne Phelps Coco, "Diseased, Maimed, Mutilated: Categorizations of Disability and an Ugly Law in Late Nineteenth-Century Chicago," *Journal of Social History* 44 (2010): 23–37. A few years ago a Christian writer for the Gospel Coalition similarly responded with disgust to gay people and wrote an article titled "The Importance of Your Gag Reflex When Discussing Homosexuality and 'Gay Marriage.'" He urged Christians to focus the debate on "sexual behavior in all its yuckiest gag-inducing truth." The author proceeded to graphically describe same-sex acts in distorted, animalistic fashion. Notably, propaganda has also been used to portray other groups as sexually deviant and therefore disgusting. African-Americans have long been dehumanized as sexually promiscuous and bestial by nature. The 1915 film *Birth of a Nation* famously portrayed black men as rampant rapists.

35. "Nashville Statement," Coalition for Biblical Sexuality, https://cbmw .org/nashville-statement.

36. My discussion on left-handedness as a problem to be fixed draws from Howard I. Kushner, *On the Other Hand: Left Hand, Right Brain, Mental Disorder, and History* (Baltimore: Johns Hopkins University Press, 2017).

37. R. Matthew Montoya, Robert S. Horton, and Jeffrey Kirchner, "Is Actual Similarity Necessary for Attraction? A Meta-Analysis of Actual and Perceived Similarity," *Journal of Social and Personal Relationships* 25 (2008): 889–922.

38. Geoffrey L. Cohen, "Party Over Policy: The Dominating Impact of Group Influence on Political Beliefs," *Journal of Personality and Social Psychology* 85 (2003): 808–22; Noshir S. Contractor and Leslie A. DeChurch, "Integrating Social Networks and Human Social Motives to Achieve Social Influence at Scale," *Proceedings of the National Academy of Sciences of the United States of America* 111 (2014): 13650–57.

39. This is not to say similarity in itself is problematic. Participating in a support group with fellow cancer survivors can be profoundly nurturing. Worshiping with other believers who share a mutual love of Christ can be a balm for the soul. Having a tribe in which to belong and collaborate helps us to survive and live life to the fullest. We need spaces where we are understood on a deep level. We need mentors and leaders who "look like us" to inspire possibilities for our own aspirations. The problem is not sameness but rather discomfort or fear of differences.

40. Both traditionalists and progressives are tempted to eradicate differences—either by "fixing" gay people through conversion treatments (traditionalists) or by deconstructing sex and gender as a way to fight oppression (progressives). Yet sexual orientation change efforts have proved largely unsuccessful. And erasure of male and female does not reduce oppression; it merely masks power dynamics in a way similar to the "love is color-blind" fallacy. Male and

female is a real thing. And so is being gay. That means the well-being of the whole will best be met by truly seeing each other.

41. Brian Brock, "Augustine's Hierarchies of Human Wholeness and Their Healing," in *Disability in the Christian Tradition: A Reader*, ed. Brian Brock and John Swinton (Grand Rapids: Eerdmans, 2012), 65–100.

42. *City of God* 16.8, quoted in Brock, "Augustine's Hierarchies," 88–89.

43. At this point, a traditionalist might ask how Scripture relates to the possibility that a same-sex orientation is harmless human variation. Without a doubt, the biblical authors were inspired. That means we need to pay attention to the nature and function of that inspiration. Significantly, the prophetic phenomenon by which they wrote did not result in omniscience. Human limitations to knowledge remained. As one example of this, the Bible includes ancient scientific perspectives on cosmology (see John H. Walton, *Genesis 1 as Ancient Cosmology* [Winona Lake, IN: Eisenbrauns, 2011]). God did not grant the biblical authors futuristic insight into astronomy, biology, or technology. That does not mean the Bible is unreliable or that we can arbitrarily pick and choose various parts as inspired. The entirety of Scripture is authoritative. But Paul makes clear that prophecy, even as a form of communication from God, results in *partial* knowledge (1 Cor. 13:9–12). The biblical authors wrote down divine truth, but they wrote it with limited knowledge.

Notes to Chapter 8

1. In addition to Focus on the Family's youth publication mentioned in the last chapter, other Christian writers advocate marrying young in light of the problem of prolonged chastity. Mark D. Regnerus, a Christian sociologist, writes, "Having to wait until age 25 or 30 to have sex *is* unreasonable [emphasis in original]. Yet if religious organizations and their adherents are going to continue advocating for Christian chastity, and I have no reason to suggest they won't or shouldn't, they must work more creatively to support younger marriages" (*Forbidden Fruit: Sex and Religion in the Lives of American Teenagers* [New York: Oxford University Press, 2007], 213).

2. "Love is color-blind" is the well-meaning but flawed belief that ignoring or pretending not to see someone's skin color will reduce racial injustice. The best way to counter oppression is not blindness but seeing someone's skin color (or sex or gender) and treating them with dignity and equity for who they are. Certain progressives who seek to deconstruct sex and gender may reject the color-blind fallacy for racism but seem unaware of how their efforts result in similar problems. Deconstruction efforts too often err by throwing the baby out with the bath water. For more on these concepts, see Adia Harvey Wingfield, "Color-Blindness Is Counterproductive," *The Atlantic*, September 13,

2015, https://www.theatlantic.com/politics/archive/2015/09/color-blindness-is
-counterproductive/405037/.

3. For leaders who continue to oppose all same-sex relationships, I offer
this final thought: be cautious about demanding a sacrifice from others that
you are not willing to make yourself. Protestants are among the few who demand celibacy from certain laypeople but prefer their leaders to be married.
The opposite is true in most other traditions and religions. The fact that many
traditionalist leaders demand lifelong celibacy from others but don't live it themselves is telling. Growing up, I heard that the sin King David committed was
that he stayed home instead of going out into battle at the front lines to lead his
soldiers. Traditionalists will say that gay marriage is destroying civilization, and
yet I know not one straight traditionalist who in his twenties, desiring marriage
and children, gave it all up to lead by example.

4. Stanton L. Jones and Mark A. Yarhouse, *Ex-Gays? A Longitudinal Study
of Religiously Mediated Change in Sexual Orientation* (Downers Grove, IL: InterVarsity Press, 2007).

5. At this stage of the study it was 15 percent. The final number was 23
percent. This was still far lower than many of us in the ex-gay world wanted to
admit, even though we regularly observed that most of us did not experience
change. We held on to hope by focusing on the few ex-gay leaders who seemed
to "make it."

6. The post, titled "Yarhouse's and Jones' Ex-Gay Study," was published on
my blog, *Pursue God*, on September 19, 2007. I closed down the blog site in 2010.
Recently, I started a new blog on sexuality at reverentsexuality.com.

Acknowledgments

In September 2017, I texted Eerdmans's editor-in-chief, James Ernest: "I don't know if you remember me, but I am wondering if you might look at a manuscript on same-sex relationships." Two years prior I had met James at a Missio Alliance conference. He invited a few authors (and would-be authors) to meet up for lunch. Somehow, I was lucky enough to be among them. At the time, I didn't have a book proposal, and my doctoral studies kept me too busy to write one. I lamented the missed opportunity to make a pitch. But I held onto James's contact information—just in case. My open door came a couple years later, during a brief break in my dissertation writing. I was blogging a series on same-sex relationships when I realized I had a book on my hands. Thankfully, James remembered me and welcomed the manuscript submission. He is the reason this book is in print. James, thank you for giving me a chance. I am so grateful.

Once my book was in the door and made it through the review process, I discovered a stellar team of people. From day one, every person I encountered at Eerdmans treated me with kindness, patience, and respect. Most of all, they were sensitive to my concerns about the editing process. Handing over my manuscript was like giving up my baby. Writing on one of the most controversial topics in the church is not easy, and I needed to know my book would be handled with care. But I needn't have worried. Lil Copan, Mary Hietbrink, and Ryan Davis were everything an author could want in editors. My book is better for their efforts. Lil, thank you for your gentle and wise feedback. You challenged me to refine this book in crucial ways. Mary, I am so grateful for your competent oversight and careful attention to my manuscript. I could always count on you to stay in close communication and answer my many questions. Ryan, you have an amazing eagle eye. Thank you for your meticulous editing and helpful comments.

I am also grateful to Rachel Brewer, publicist at Eerdmans. Thank you for caring about my book and helping me to get the word out.

Special thanks go to Brian Hui and Gene Schlesinger, who read the manuscript in full before it even went to the publisher. You are both such dear brothers. Thank you for being there for me. I am also grateful for friends and colleagues who reviewed portions of this manuscript, including Kirsten Guidero, Kyle Potter, and J. (who asked to remain anonymous). Thanks also to Wesley Hill, my iron-sharpens-iron friend, for constructive feedback. And I am grateful to Mark Yarhouse for reading the section on "The Science of Same-Sex Attraction" to verify its accuracy.

This book is the product of many years of study and reflection within community, including a two-month discernment process with thirteen people during the summer of 2013. I am still amazed that so many people would gift me with their presence while I searched for answers. So, thank you, Brian, Johanna, Mark, Kirsten, Oliver, Steve, Julie, Jennifer, Wade, Curtis, Jeff, Darin, and Wesley.

My church community in Durham has blessed me with friendship, unconditional love, and support. I am particularly grateful for my weekly CityWell home group, as well as the group As We Are.

And last but not least, my sister. Crystal, thank you for your willingness to ask hard questions. I love you.

Subject-Name Index

Adam. *See* creation; fall, of
humankind
attraction. *See* same-sex attraction, causation of
Augustine
on fall, 86, 98–99, 113
on marriage, 78
on Rom. 1, 23

Butterfield, Rosaria, 12–13, 84–85

celibacy
early Christian views of, 21, 34,
36, 70, 75–79, 80
expectation of, 10–11, 13, 67, 68,
71, 73, 80n28, 97, 100, 101,
105n3
feasibility of, traditionalist
views on, 11, 68, 71n6,
73–74, 80, 103, 104–5
infeasibility of, pastoral responses to, 66–67, 68–71,
79, 80, 81–82, 95, 104–5
celibate gay movement, 9–12, 13,
14, 111
Chambers, Alan, 6, 9n31, 10, 12, 72

Chrysostom, John, 1–2
Clement of Alexandria, 2
complementarity
anatomical, progressive views
on, 24, 25, 30–32, 33–35,
39–41, 104, 106
anatomical, traditionalist views
on, 20, 24, 25–27, 29–30,
56, 104, 105
early Jewish and Greco-Roman
views on, 19n9, 35n13
gender, progressive views on,
35n13, 39–41
gender, traditionalist views on,
20, 27–28, 29–30, 56
See also sexual differentiation
contrary to nature. *See* unnatural
covenant/covenanted. *See* marriage
creation
ordinance, application of, 54,
58, 63, 64–66, 83, 102, 114
progressive interpretation of,
30–33, 37, 38, 40, 41, 43,
80, 98–99, 106, 113
science, in relation to, 85–88,
98–99

traditionalist interpretation of, 26–27, 28, 29, 30n6, 40, 43

desire
early Christian views on 1–2, 39n20, 76, 77n23
progressive arguments about, 36, 38–39, 97, 106
strong, 76, 78–79, 80, 82, 104–5
traditionalist arguments about, 28, 83, 84–85, 104–5
See also lust; same-sex attraction, causation of
differentiation, 77, 94
divorce
evangelicals on ethics of, 69–70, 80–81, 82, 103
Jesus and biblical authors on, 26–27, 31–32, 33, 61–63, 80n30

ethics
applicability of biblical laws for, 43–45, 50–52, 54, 55–58, 66, 102–3, 106
biblical authors' approach to, 20, 58–66, 68, 69, 106
deliberative process for deriving from Scripture, 51–52, 58–67, 68–70, 80–82, 83, 102–3
ex-gay movement
challenges of, 9–10, 11, 109–10
history of, 6–8, 12, 14
Exodus International
effectiveness of, 71–72
history of 6–8, 9, 10, 11, 12

fall, of humankind
Adam and human origins, in relation to, 83, 85–88, 99
human variation not resulting from, 84, 85, 88, 97–100

moral consequences of, 83–85, 88–89
natural consequences of, 83–85, 89–90, 95–97, 99–100
See also same-sex attraction, causation of: the fall in relation to
female same-sex relations, 2n12, 17, 19, 22–23, 29, 92
fertility. *See* infertile/non-procreative; procreation

gay people, negative caricatures of
criminal, 4–5, 6, 101
mentally ill or diseased, 2–3, 4–5, 7–8, 14, 70, 98, 101
spiritually depraved, 1–2, 4–5, 14, 70, 88–89, 91, 101, 108
See also lust
gay rights, 3, 4, 6, 8, 14, 91–92, 104
gender norms, in antiquity, 17, 18, 19, 20, 22, 23, 35n13, 36, 106. *See also* complementarity

Henry, Matthew, 2
Hill, Wesley, 9n31, 11, 12, 70, 84–85

identity, 2n13, 13
idolatry, 2, 17, 19, 36–37, 38–39, 41, 56
infertile/non-procreative, 19n9, 27, 34–35, 36, 106
inspiration, biblical, 16, 43–44, 45, 50, 52, 55, 58–59, 61, 65, 99n43

Josephus
on causes of same-sex desire, 19n9
on pederasty, 17–18
on procreation, 19n9, 22, 28

law, Israelite
  ancient Near Eastern law, in
    comparison to, 16–17,
    45–50, 55
  Jesus's interpretation of, 31–32,
    52, 57, 61–62, 63–64, 65,
    66, 68, 102
  Paul's interpretation of, 56, 57,
    61n16, 65–66, 68, 80n30
  same-sex relations in, 16, 17, 22,
    43, 44, 51–52, 55, 102, 106
  significance of, 43–45, 45n2,
    51–52, 55
  See also ethics
lesbian. See female same-sex
  relations
Lewis, C. S., 3
lust, 1–2, 18, 19, 20, 22, 23, 36, 84,
  91, 97, 106
Luther, Martin
  on causes of same-sex desire, 2
  on celibacy and marriage,
    78–79, 105

marriage
  early Christian and Jewish
    perspectives of, 1n2, 21–22,
    30n6, 32n10, 69, 75–76,
    77–79
  necessity of, 10, 74, 75, 76,
    77–79, 80, 81–82, 103n1
  progressive views on, 20, 30–35,
    39–40, 41, 43, 57–58, 69,
    70, 80, 82, 83, 96–97, 102,
    104, 106
  traditionalist views on, 20,
    21, 24, 26–28, 29–30, 35,
    40–41, 66, 70, 104–5
  See also mixed orientation
    marriage
medical theories, of same-sex
  attraction. See same-sex
  attraction, causation of

mixed orientation marriage, 11, 71,
  91n19, 97, 100, 110
Moberly, Elizabeth, 7

nature/natural, 19n9, 22, 23,
  28, 35n13, 36. See also
  unnatural
Nicolosi, Joseph, 5, 7

orientation. See sexual orientation, change

para physin. See unnatural
passion. See desire; lust
pederasty, 17–18, 19, 20, 23, 29
peer same-sex relations, in antiquity, 16n1, 17, 18, 20
Philo
  on causes of same-sex desire, 2,
    19n9, 36
  on pederasty, 17–18
  on procreation, 19n9, 21–22, 28
Plato, 2, 17, 18, 30n6, 36
procreation
  early Jewish and Christian
    views on, 19, 21–23, 35–36,
    75, 77, 86
  the fall in relation to, 86, 88
  Greco-Roman views on, 18,
    19n9, 23
  progressive views on, 33–36, 41
  traditionalist views on, 20, 26,
    27, 28–29
prostitution, male-male, 17, 18, 19,
  20, 23, 29
psychological theories, of same-
  sex attraction. See same-
  sex attraction, causation of

reparative therapy, 7, 12, 92n20

same-sex attraction, causation of
  the fall in relation to, 13, 28,

36–37, 38–39, 83–85,
88–90, 95, 97–100
medical or scientific theories,
ancient, 2, 2n13
medical or scientific theories,
modern, 2–3, 7, 8, 9, 11, 12,
72, 91–94, 97–100
See also desire; sexual orientation, change
sexual differentiation
early church fathers' views of,
77
scientific discussion of, 94
See also complementarity
sexual identity, 2n13, 13
sexual orientation, change
progressive claims related to,
91–92

scientific evidence related to, 7,
71–73
traditionalist claims related to,
2, 3, 6–7, 8, 9–10, 11, 12–13,
14, 72n12, 109–11
See also reparative therapy;
same-sex attraction,
causation of
slaves
Israelite law concerning, 48,
59–61, 63, 64, 102
sex with, 18, 19, 23, 29, 32n10

unnatural, 2, 19, 22, 23, 28, 29, 35,
36, 106. *See also* nature/
natural

Worthen, Frank, 6, 7, 10

Scripture Index

OLD TESTAMENT

Genesis

1	21, 25, 26, 33, 35, 37
1–2	29, 41
1–3	25, 40, 56
1:11–12	21
1:21–22	21
1:23	28
1:24–25	21
1:26	23n14, 28
1:26–27	28, 31, 36, 37n17
1:27	26, 28, 31
1:28	21, 75
2	30, 32, 40
2:1–3	65
2:16–18	30
2:18	27, 30
2:20	30
2:23	30
2:24	26, 27, 31–32, 33
3	28, 37, 85–86, 87
3:22–23	87n9
6:5	90
29:14	31
38:6–10	32n10

Exodus

19:14–15	75
19:18–21:11	61
20:2–17	46
20:10–11	65
21–23	46
21:2–11	59
21:7	61
21:22–25	48
21:28–30	47
24:14–15	49
31:12–15	65
31:16–17	65
31:17	65
34:10–26	47

Leviticus

11:9–12	44
17–26	46
18:3	19
18:22	17, 19, 43
18:23	22
18:24	19
18:30	19
19:14	55
20:13	17, 19, 43
20:16	22
20:23	19
21:13–15	23
24:5–9	64

Deuteronomy

4:16–18	37n17
5:6–21	46
12–26	46, 61n17
15:12–18	60–61, 102
16:18–19	50
22	43
22:28–29	32n10, 102, 106
23:17–18	17
24:1–4	61n17, 62, 80
24:17	51
27:19	51
28:4	21
28:11	21
28:18	21
28:41	21
28:51	21
28:53	21

28:56–57	21	19:4–6	26	**Romans**		
28:63	21	19:9	62	1	2, 18, 22, 25, 28,	
38:8–10	21	19:10–12	76		29, 35, 36–39, 41	
				1–2	38	
1 Samuel		**Mark**		1:19–20	37	
1:8	33	2:27	65	1:20	28	
21:4	75	7:21	90	1:21	38	
		10	30	1:21–22	37	
2 Samuel		10:1–9	25, 26	1:23	28, 37n17, 38	
13	51	10:2–12	31, 61	1:24–32	38	
25:39–43	32n10	10:4	31	1:26–27	19, 28	
		10:5	61	1:27	19, 23	
Psalms		10:6	31	2:1	38	
14	90	10:6–8	63	2:11	38	
51:5	77	10:8	32	3:9–20	90	
58:3	90	10:9	32	5	85–86, 87	
82:3	51	10:11–12	32, 62	5:12	86	
85:10	51	16:1	65	5:14	87–88	
89:14	50			13:8–10	57	
97:11	51	**Luke**		14:21–23	67n17	
		4:16	65			
Proverbs		11:41	57	**1 Corinthians**		
4:18	51	12:47–48	67n17	6:9–10	18, 19	
26:4–5	67n21	18:29–30	76	6:12–20	76	
		20:34	76	7:1	76	
Isaiah		20:34–36	34, 75–76	7:2–5	76	
1:17	51	23:34	67n17	7:5	67n17, 75, 76	
2:9 11	59			7:9	67n17, 69, 76, 105	
11:8	75	**John**		7:12–13	70	
32:17	51	5:5–9	64	7:12–15	62	
58	65	9:1–3	3	7:15	69	
		9:2	96	7:29	77	
Malachi		9:41	67n17	7:32–35	76	
4:2	51	16:21	21	7:36	67n17, 76	
				7:37	32n10	
		Acts		13:9–12	61n16,	
NEW TESTAMENT		6:1–4	81		99n43	
		10:12	37n17	14:45	88	
Matthew		11:6	37n17			
12:3–4	63	17:1–2	65	**Galatians**		
12:9–13	64	18:4	65	3:28	56	
12:12	64			5:6	57	
19:1–6	25			5:22–23	56	

Ephesians

5	29, 40, 41
5:22–32	25
5:25	29, 40
5:25–32	39
5:28	40
5:28–29	70
5:29	40
5:29–32	29
5:31	40
6:1–4	21

Colossians

2:8–23	65
2:16–17	66
3:20	21

1 Thessalonians

5:17	77

1 Timothy

1:9–10	18, 19
2:12	54
2:12–15	32n10
2:15	21

Hebrews

4:8–11	76
10:1	66

1 John

4:12	57

Revelation

14:1–5	75
19:7–9	25, 29
21:1–3	76
21:3–4	66

APOCRYPHAL BOOKS

Wisdom of Solomon

2:24	87n9
3:13	75
3:13b–4:6	21n10
13–14	37
13:1	37
13:7–9	37